Introduction

The story of *Wild Caught and Close to Home* begins in the cool, deep waters of the Great Lakes.

The Great Lakes are the largest freshwater system in the world, with over 95,000 square miles of surface area and 20 percent of the world's surface fresh water. These waters are home to many fish species that have sustained the people of the Great Lakes region for centuries. At the top of that list is Great Lakes whitefish (*Coregonus clupeaformis*).

Each catch that fishermen haul in represents generations of experience and commitment to the trade. They use trap nets and gill nets on the open water to pull in the whitefish bounty. Much of the fish is then processed locally to sell at markets and retail outlets in the region.

The silvery fish weighs an average of 2–4 pounds and has a sweet, light flavor, making it the perfect portion and perfect base protein on which to build a delicious, nutritious meal. Great Lakes whitefish are a good source of omega-3 fatty acids, B6, B12, and other vitamins and minerals.

This Great Lakes whitefish cookbook is the result of Michigan Sea Grant's ongoing efforts to educate the public about this signature, native species. In collecting the recipes for this book, we trolled the Great Lakes and met with restaurant chefs, fishermen and culinary educators from Illinois, Michigan and Minnesota. We requested their prized recipes to showcase a variety of cookery methods. The result, as you are about to experience, is a fantastic compilation of the creative works of lake whitefish cooking experts.

While this book focuses on lake whitefish, we hope it becomes a general resource for you. Any of these recipes can be adapted using your favorite fishes. Each section of the book covers different preparation methods and offers a sampling of recipes that use the highlighted techniques.

People who love fish tend to get in a rut, using the same recipes over and over. We hope this book will prompt folks to try different methods for cooking, pairing these recipes with their own tastes and creativity. People who have hesitated to prepare lake whitefish because of fish-cookery fear, or those who may think lake whitefish is boring, will find the recipes in this book delicious and easy to follow.

We hope the story ends with this treasured Great Lakes fish gaining the recognition it deserves.

EDITORS

Chef Deborah Pearce, CHE
Chef Chris Kibit, CCE, CHE

For more detailed information about Great Lakes whitefish history, as well as fishing family and additional chef profiles and recipes, visit www.greatlakeswhitefish.com

Table of Contents

ROASTING AND BAKING

SMOKING AND PICKLING

ACKNOWLEDGEMENTS

Many people were involved in producing this publication. We are deeply grateful to Chef Deborah Pearce who suggested this cookbook and who has contributed so much to its creation — soliciting and creating recipes, expertly preparing food for photography, patiently explaining culinary terms, and making necessary adjustments. We especially thank Chef Chris Kibit, who also solicited and screened recipes from colleagues and contributed some of his own favorites. Both of these culinary educators developed the techniques material. We appreciate all the chefs and cooks who contributed recipes and gave so freely of their expertise. Finally, we admire and value the contribution of Michigan commercial fishing families and related businesses who commit their time, energy, knowledge and skill to catching, processing and delivering Great Lakes whitefish to benefit all of us.

PROJECT PERSONNEL

Project Director:
Charles Pistis

Project Coordinator:
Carol Swinehart

Creative Direction:
Elizabeth LaPorte
Todd Marsee

Writers:
Stephanie Ariganello
Chef Christopher Kibit
Ronald E. Kinnunen
Chef Deborah Pearce
Carol Swinehart

Photographers:
Big Event Studios –
   Julie Line, Rob Hunter and
   Loretta Gorman (Food Stylist)
Christina Carson
Elizabeth LaPorte
Todd Marsee
Sharon Moen
Andrew Muir
Brandon Schroeder
Carol Swinehart
Yin Tang

Graphic Designer:
Todd Marsee

Editors:
Stephanie Ariganello
Carol Swinehart

Reviewers:
Ronald E. Kinnunen
Charles Pistis

Transcriber:
Marcia Baar

Account Manager:
Pam Bailey

Contributing Chefs and Cooks

Many of the recipes in this book were contributed by credentialed, experienced chefs and by fishing families who have been preparing Great Lakes whitefish for generations. The following pages provide brief introductions to these generous folks. For more information about them and other Great Lakes chefs, please visit www.greatlakeswhitefish.com

DALE BEAUBIEN, Executive Chef

Restaurant 301, Duluth Sheraton Hotel, Duluth, Minnesota

RECIPE: Whitefish Saltimbocca

Chef Dale Beaubien comes from one of Detroit's founding families and learned to appreciate good cooking as a child, watching babysitters make fresh ravioli and warm, buttered tortillas. He calls himself a Great Lakes boy, and Great Lakes whitefish is an important part of that. He says, "The lake is right there, so it just makes sense to have whitefish on the menu. The flavor is not too 'fishy,' and it holds up well to whatever method you choose to cook it." It has definitely been a popular item at the restaurants where he's worked. At one Marquette establishment, they'd go through 50 pounds in a weekend. His recipe for saltimbocca combines the fish and Italian ham with a wine sauce for an especially mellow flavor.

JILL BENTGEN, Proprietor

Mackinac Straits Fish Company, St. Ignace, Michigan

RECIPES: Smoked Fish Pasta Salad; Mustard Dill Sauce

Jill Bentgen had a career with a Fortune 500 consumer products company before her native Upper Peninsula called her home, where she has applied her knowledge, skills and experience in a new way. Mackinac Straits Fish Company is the channel through which she distributes fresh and fresh-frozen Great Lakes whitefish fillets and other products such as *White Caps*, a smoked lake whitefish spread. She chooses her sources carefully and adds value to raw fish by smoking it, producing sausage and making spreads. She sells those items as branded products that customers recognize for their quality.

HANS BURTSCHER, Executive Chef, Vice President of Food and Beverage

Grand Hotel, Mackinac Island, Michigan

RECIPE: Mackinac Whitefish Bisque

Originally from Austria, Chef Hans Burtscher presides over food and beverage operations at the venerable, world-renowned Grand Hotel that attracts guests from many countries. Whether preparing for a banquet or designing a dining room menu to delight discriminating palates, he thinks the simplest preparation is the best for whitefish. His contribution to this cookbook marries two favorite Great Lakes fishes — lake whitefish and lake trout. "The nice thing is that we have fisheries that are right here. We love using Michigan products because they're local and fresh."

PAUL CARLSON, Chef

The Hearth and Vine, Black Star Farms, Suttons Bay, Michigan

RECIPE: Cedar Plank-Roasted Whitefish with Roasted Tomato and Olive Relish

Chef Paul Carlson comes from a long line of cooks, gleaning a lot from his grandfather. Now he's learning to make the most of the wood-fired oven and steam kettle at The Hearth and Vine, where he develops and prepares tasty, satisfying, crowd-pleasing dishes. He's served nationally known chef colleagues, as well as thousands of other visitors at this agricultural destination. The nearby vineyards and organic garden provide many opportunities to try different flavor combinations with Great Lakes whitefish, which he considers a blank canvas. You will need some cedar planks, but you don't need a wood-fired oven or an adjacent vineyard to prepare Chef Carlson's classic roasted whitefish.

JACK J. DELBY, Executive Chef

Renaissance Schaumburg Hotel and Convention Center, Schaumburg, Illinois

RECIPE: Seared Whitefish with Lemon Rémoulade and German Fingerling Potato Salad

Chef Jack Delby says, "It is important to do what you love and enjoy it. When you're happy, everyone else is." Being critiqued by other chefs is easy compared with trying to get his wife's culinary blessing. "If she says it's good, I know it's cool to serve it to just about anybody." He served the dish in this cookbook to hundreds of his colleagues, using a warm vinaigrette on the roasted potatoes and a lemon rémoulade on the plate with it. Delby appreciates the versatility of Great Lakes whitefish. "You can stuff it, roll it, poach it and broil it. I also like the way it smokes and cures."

TOM SPAULDING AND JOHN GAUTHIER, Co-owners

Gauthier & Spaulding Fisheries, Rogers City, Michigan

RECIPES: Blackened Whitefish; Homestyle Whitefish Loaf; Roy and Alice's Pickled Fish; Whitefish Marinade; Barbecued Whitefish Fillets

John Gauthier's family has been fishing the Great Lakes for more than 100 years. He was about 10 years old when he started working gill net tugs in northern Lake Michigan. Now, he and his business partner Tom Spaulding fish trap nets in northern Lake Huron, and they are founding members of a whitefish marketing cooperative. They produce perfectly pin-boned whitefish fillets and whitefish cakes under the co-op's strict standards and sell them as *Legends of the Lakes*™. Meanwhile, they have collected many tried-and-true recipes for preparing this commercially harvested species and want others to enjoy them, too.

ROBIN HOLMES, Executive Chef

Pacinos Restaurant at the Best Western, Escanaba, Michigan

RECIPES: Whitefish in Foil ala Veracruzana; Great Lakes Whitefish Milano; Smoked Great Lakes Whitefish and Artichoke Dip

Chef Robin Holmes started his cooking career in an Upper Peninsula (Michigan) pasty shop, at one time helping to produce 15,000 of the popular 'pocket' meals in 24 hours. While living in Minnesota and California, he had to have his 'whitefish fix' whenever he came home for a visit. Great Lakes whitefish has always been a staple on the menu of local restaurants, but he's been developing non-traditional recipes to keep it interesting. "It is such a great product and so easy to cook. You can do so many things with it without masking its delicate, clean flavor."

CHRIS KIBIT, CEC, CHE, Professor

Hospitality Management Program, Northern Michigan University, Marquette, Michigan

RECIPES: Herbed Whitefish en Papillote; Sautéed Great Lakes Whitefish Livers Marsala; Spicy Whitefish Rounds

Chef Chris Kibit has been in the hospitality industry for 30 years, and he has cooked for three recent Michigan State University presidents, preparing food for three very different families and their guests. Now he is a professor at Northern Michigan University, educating the next generation of chefs and learning more about Great Lakes whitefish. "Cooking is something that I love. I teach now, but I still cook. I love to teach it because I feel that a lot of people helped me, and now it is my turn to pass it on." Whatever the preparation, "Fresh is always best, but fresh isn't always possible and well-frozen fish, such as *Legends of the Lakes*™ fillets, is also a great product."

DARLENE KLINE, Private Chef and Caterer

Grand Affairs Catering, Charlevoix, Michigan

RECIPE: Smoked Whitefish Cakes with a Sweet Cherry Coulis

The atmosphere at Morgan's Tavern in Horton Bay, Michigan, is very reminiscent of its most famous patron — Ernest Hemmingway. One can just imagine him having a cold beer at the bar and enjoying a fish snack. Chef Darlene Kline likes nothing better than to see folks gather at the tables there while she prepares smoked whitefish cakes as part of the tavern's tapas menu. The tavern is one of the local establishments where Kline exercises her culinary skills. She's adopted the philosophy of a chef mentor who taught her how important it is to teach someone else what you know. She developed the dish in this book to incorporate many fresh flavors that complement Great Lakes whitefish.

JEFF KUDRNA, Executive Chef

Clearbrook Golf Course, Saugatuck, Michigan

RECIPES: Broiled Whitefish with Caper Berry Aioli; Smoked Whitefish Dip with Ale

Chicago native Chef Jeff Kudrna didn't know much about Great Lakes whitefish until he went to Northern Michigan University and worked in local restaurants where whitefish is a menu must. Now he's an executive chef and a master at pin-boning whitefish fillets. His current clientele can't get enough of the species. He says, "It's the fish for people who don't like fish and a treat for those who do." He likes food that no one else has handled, whether from the local fish purveyor or the herb garden he's planted just outside his restaurant kitchen. He's provided two popular examples of the many ways he prepares Great Lakes whitefish.

CYNTHIA MANNING, Sous Chef

Shaw Hall, Michigan State University, East Lansing, Michigan

RECIPES: Smoked Whitefish Salad; Potato-Encrusted Whitefish

Sous Chef Cynthia Manning's cooking resume includes a college fraternity, a university dining service, and chef to two Michigan governors as well as the president of Michigan State University. At the governor's mansion on Mackinac Island, she found the local, fresh Great Lakes whitefish catch easy to work with. One governor's wife especially liked her whitefish salad. Now serving hundreds of college students every day, she's finding that whitefish appeals to them. "Today's student has a much more sophisticated palate than students from 15–20 years ago." The salad and potato-encrusted whitefish she contributed to this book appear on her "Michigan products" menu.

NATHAN MILESKI, Corporate Executive Chef

Northern Michigan University, Marquette, Michigan

RECIPES: Thai Whitefish Hor Mok; Fried Whitefish Tacos; Black Pepper and Sea Salt Whitefish and Chips with Lemon-Tarragon Aioli; Marquette Whitefish Chowder

Men in the Mileski family love to cook, so it came naturally to Nathan. He attended the Culinary Institute of America in New York City. After graduation, he worked in Minnesota, but found his way back home to Michigan's Upper Peninsula. Now he's at Northern Michigan University, where he oversees multiple operations across campus. Nathan enjoys incorporating Great Lakes whitefish in his menus because of its versatility, but likes to do traditional dishes with his own flair.

RAJEEV PATGAONKAR, Executive Sous Chef

Kellogg Hotel and Conference Center, Michigan State University, East Lansing, Michigan

RECIPES: Chardonnay-Poached Great Lakes Whitefish with Couscous; Pistachio-Crusted Great Lakes Whitefish with Citrus Spinach Salad

Chef Rajeev Patgaonkar was a somewhat rebellious young man in his native India. He didn't want to become a doctor or engineer like his brothers and sisters. Chef Rajeev wanted a career as unique as he was. He cooked for the royal family of Saudi Arabia and for the Sultan of Oman before joining Carnival Cruise Lines. He now uses all that experience as executive sous chef at Michigan State University's Kellogg Hotel and Conference Center. He notes how healthy the pistachio-crusted preparation is — not grilled or fried.

DEBORAH PEARCE, CHE, Assistant Professor

Hospitality Management Program, Northern Michigan University, Marquette, Michigan

RECIPES: Great Lakes Whitefish Court Bouillon; Great Lakes Summer Whitefish

Growing up on the East Coast and enjoying her mother's and grandmother's cooking with fresh, local ingredients, Chef Deborah Pearce never imagined that she would become a chef, let alone a culinary educator. After training at the Culinary Institute of America in New York City and with over 20 years' experience as a chef in the U.S. Virgin Islands, she agreed to head north to Michigan's Upper Peninsula, where she's been sharing her culinary knowledge and skills with students in Northern Michigan University's Hospitality Management Program. She has learned a lot about Great Lakes whitefish and how local folks prepare it, collecting and adapting favorite recipes and using the abundance of ingredients indigenous to the area.

CHRIS STURZL, CEC, CCE, CSCE, Executive Chef

Champlin Park High School, Champlin, Minnesota

RECIPE: Teriyaki Bacon-Wrapped Whitefish

As a high school teacher, Chef Chris Sturzl gives tests, but he's also learned to take them… from his chef colleagues. He's passed the CEC (Certified Executive Chef) exam and was chosen 2009 Chef of the Year by American Culinary Federation peers in Minnesota's Twin Cities. He learned about cooking in college home economics courses, and he's also learned hospitality management from working in restaurants. Cooking has become so popular in recent years, undoubtedly influenced by television cooking shows, that students are on a waiting list to take his elective culinary cuisine classes. Sturzl considers Great Lakes whitefish a "bread and butter" fish, a staple in the regional diet. He prepares it several different ways, one of which he's sharing in this book.

TED THILL, Owner

Thill's Fish House, Marquette, Michigan

RECIPES: Thill's Fish House Smoked Whitefish Spread; Grandpa Thill's Whitefish Chowder

You'll find whitefish from Thill's on the menu of Marquette's finest restaurants. You may also buy it fresh or smoked at their retail shop on the waterfront. Their trap net boat is docked right behind it, a symbol of a family that's all about fishing. Ted's sons are carrying on the tradition, and his grandsons are interested, too. It's easy to understand how several generations of Thills have developed favorite recipes such as the ones in this book. Ted says: "If you don't have celery seed, don't even think of making Grandpa's chowder." But you can easily find it at most supermarkets, so get some and give it a try.

ERIC VILLEGAS, Chef/Host

Fork in the Road Television Show, Williamston, Michigan

RECIPE: Great Lakes Muffaletta

As host of the Emmy Award-winning cooking show "Fork in the Road," Eric Villegas capitalizes on his knowledge of Michigan foods, as well as his outgoing personality. One of his favorite Michigan foods is Great Lakes whitefish, as demonstrated by the number of whitefish dishes in the cookbook named for the show. "When somebody says whitefish, I automatically think of the Great Lakes. Other than pasties, I don't think anything represents Michigan better than whitefish." His muffaletta shows off the smoked flavor and texture whitefish can provide.

Purchasing, Handling and Health Benefits of Great Lakes Whitefish

IT'S GOOD TO BE FROM THE GREAT LAKES

Great Lakes whitefish come from the largest freshwater lake system in the world. This results in several important benefits.

WILD VS. FARMED - Most chefs and cooks believe that wild-caught fish offer superior flavor and texture to farmed fish. Wild Great Lakes whitefish is found only in cold, northern waters. Reputable brands guarantee that their fish is accurately labeled "Wild Caught from the Great Lakes - Product of U.S.A."

FROZEN VS. FRESH - Studies show that when fresh fish is carefully vacuum packed, frozen and expertly handled, it keeps flavor and texture that is "fresh from the water." Tests with consumer panels at Michigan State University's Department of Food Science and Human Nutrition Sensory Evaluation Laboratory concluded that consumers could not differentiate between the cooked flavor of fresh lake whitefish and vacuum packed, frozen lake whitefish. The nutritional value of fresh and frozen fish is very similar.

A MATTER OF DISTANCE - Great Lakes whitefish from Michigan's scientifically managed fisheries is caught by small, family-based operations and processed in the Great Lakes area, reducing its carbon footprint and increasing its sustainability. This fish makes no journeys to and from Asia for processing (unlike other fish). When purchasing fish, look for the USDA-required country of origin label and also check where it was processed.

GREAT LAKES WHITEFISH HEALTH PROFILE

Great Lakes whitefish boasts a long list of health advantages, including being a source of high-quality, low-cost protein with beneficial omega-3 fatty acids, vitamins and minerals. Medical professionals encourage most people to eat fish twice a week.

OMEGA-3S - One 3-ounce serving of Great Lakes whitefish features omega-3 fatty acids: .35g of EPA and 1.03g of DHA, to be exact. That's more than pink and sockeye salmon. Supportive but inconclusive research shows that consuming EPA and DHA omega-3 fatty acids may reduce the risk of coronary heart disease.

VITAMINS - A 3-ounce serving of Great Lakes whitefish is a good source of niacin plus vitamins B6 and B12. It also contains small amounts of thiamine, riboflavin, folate and vitamins A and E.

MINERALS - Three ounces of Great Lakes whitefish count as an "excellent source" of phosphorus and selenium and a "good source" of potassium, along with small amounts of calcium, iron and zinc.

NUTRITION FACTS

8 ounce serving (224 grams)	
Calories 300	
Total Fat (grams) 13	Sodium (mg) 114
Saturated Fat (grams) 2	Total Carbohydrate (grams) 0
Cholesterol (mg) 134	Dietary fiber (grams) 0
	Sugar (grams) 0
	Protein (grams) 43

PURCHASING FRESH GREAT LAKES WHITEFISH

This is, of course, the optimal way to cook whitefish. In fact, in cultures where fish is a staple of the diet, people prize freshness so highly that some will refuse any fish that has been out of the water more than 6 hours. With proper care and handling, this selectivity is not necessary. It is important to know how to choose fresh fish. Always buy from a reputable fish merchant.

Fresh Great Lakes whitefish flesh is firm and springs back when pressed gently; it has not begun separating from the bones. Fillets are moist and firm and look freshly cut, having no traces of browning around the edges nor a dried out look. The whitefish, whole or fillets, should be clean-smelling and mild, some say like fresh cucumbers. The skin of the fish should be silvery and shiny.

You may be able to buy Great Lakes whitefish in a variety of forms.

- **Whole** – with head intact and tail and fins attached. The eyes of a whole fish should be clear, full and often protruding. The gills should be bright red and free of slime.
  - Dressed fish are gutted and scaled with the head, tail and fins intact.
  - Pan-dressed fish have the head and tail cut off so that the fish fits more easily into a skillet.
- **Fillet** – boneless portion of fish with skin on, skin off, or pin-boned. Pin-boned fillets have all of the smallest bones removed. Whitefish fillets most often come with the skin on, but you may ask the fish purveyor to remove it to suit your taste or recipe, or you may skin it yourself, following the steps shown below.

1. Place the fish on a cutting board, skin-side down.
2. Grasping the tail end of the fillet, carefully insert the knife between the skin and the fish flesh.
3. Hold the skin and slide the knife slowly down the length of the fillet.

- **Livers** – considered by many to be a delicacy, these may be available from the fish merchant if you call and ask.
- **Caviar or Roe** – the orange-gold, salty caviar may also be available from fish retailers upon request.

HANDLING GREAT LAKES WHITEFISH

STORING FROZEN GREAT LAKES WHITEFISH

You can safely store well-wrapped whitefish fillets in the freezer at 0°F or below for about 3 months.

THAWING FROZEN GREAT LAKES WHITEFISH

If your recipe calls for thawed fillets, defrost them in the refrigerator overnight in their original packaging. You can also defrost under cold running water or place in a bowl of cold water (change water every 30 minutes). If you are planning to cook immediately, you may defrost fillets in the microwave (should be icy but pliable). Thaw only what you expect to use; never re-freeze previously frozen fish. Defrosted fillets can be stored in plastic wrap, well chilled (32 degrees) for up to 2 days before using. Keep them in the coldest part of the refrigerator.

COOKING FROZEN GREAT LAKES WHITEFISH

Great Lakes whitefish fillets may be baked, broiled or microwaved right from the freezer, before they start to drip moisture. Bake or broil longer at a slightly lower temperature. An extra 10 minutes for each inch of thickness should suffice.

STORING FRESH GREAT LAKES WHITEFISH

Fresh fish are known for being perishable. By following these simple guidelines you should have no problem keeping and cooking the freshest of Great Lakes whitefish. Still, remember, when in doubt, throw it out.

- If you purchase the fish whole (not dressed), clean and gut before storing.
- Place in a leak-proof wrapper as soon as possible after purchasing or catching.
- Keep whitefish refrigerated (35°–40°F). If you must hold the fish before refrigerating, store it in a perforated pan over ice in a cooler (not resting directly on the ice to prevent burning) as long as the temperature remains around 35°–40°F.
- Cook fresh whitefish within 2 days. Once cooked, you can keep the fish in the refrigerator, covered, for 2 or 3 more days at most.

Purchasing, Handling and Health Benefits of Great Lakes Whitefish

ROOM TEMPERATURE ADVISORY

If your recipe calls for the fish to be at room temperature for optimum cooking (such as in various frying methods), you should not keep it out of the refrigerator or freezer for more than 2 hours, including the time necessary to thaw or bring it to room temperature.

WHEN IS IT DONE?

Here are 3 simple ways to tell when your Great Lakes whitefish is fully cooked:

- The flesh is opaque.
- When you insert a fork, the flesh easily flakes apart.
- The fish is slightly firm to the touch.

NOTES

FRIED WHITEFISH TACOS

Frying Techniques

Frying, whether deep frying or pan frying, is one of the most popular fish preparation techniques. The goal of frying is to produce a crisp, golden-brown crust while maintaining a moist interior. This high-heat method seals in the juices and cooks the fish rapidly, lending itself beautifully to most fish. Frying may be healthier than you think. Maintaining the high temperature of the frying oil will reduce absorption of it into the breading and fish. Using a vegetable oil such as canola also contributes to a healthier end result.

The fish for either method of frying should be less than an inch thick. Fish to be fried are usually covered with a batter or breading. Many commercial fish batter and breading products are available.

Batters consist of dry ingredients such as flour or cornstarch in conjunction with liquids like milk, beer or water. Herbs, spices, cheese, grated onion, garlic or ginger blended into the batter can further enhance the flavor.

Breading can be as simple as dusting the food in flour or using a standard breading procedure. The standard breading procedure involves 3 steps: first, dust the food in flour, (take care to shake off the excess); then dip it in beaten eggs; and finally, dredge it in bread crumbs or some other form of outer coating. Season the food with salt and pepper prior to coating. Allowing the food to rest for 15–30 minutes before frying enables the breading to stick better.

When frying fish, it is important to remember to maintain the temperature of the fat or oil. Adding fish to hot oil will drop the temperature of the oil. The colder the fish, the more the oil temperature will drop. Allow refrigerated fish to warm to room temperature before introducing it to the oil. Be sure not to overload the pan or fryer as this will also affect the temperature and quality of cooking. Monitor the temperature and make adjustments accordingly as you cook, raising or lowering the temperature as needed. Oil for frying should be in the 350°–375°F range. Deep frying is almost always done in some form of vegetable oil.

DEEP FRYING

Equipment

☐ Electric deep fryer or Dutch oven
☐ Heavy frying pan with sides at least 2 inches high
☐ Thermometer
☐ Slotted spoon or long-handled tongs
☐ Rack for draining
☐ Paper towels

In deep frying, fish is cooked in a deep fryer or heavy-gauge frying pan with sides at least 2 inches high with enough oil to completely submerge the fish. The fish is coated with a seasoned batter or breading just prior to frying.

Preheat the oil to 350°F. It is also a good idea to test the oil with a small amount of batter before cooking the fish. If it's the correct temperature, the oil will sizzle immediately. Lower the fish into the oil slowly to avoid splatters and loss of breading. The fish should 'swim' in the oil and should be turned once to ensure both sides are equally golden brown.

If the proper temperature has been maintained, your fish should be done at this point to golden brown. As soon as the food is cooked, remove it. Place it on draining rack over a plate covered with paper towel to further decrease oil absorption. Keep in a warm oven if you need to cook additional batches. Serve immediately.

PAN FRYING

Equipment:

☐ Heavy skillet with high sides
☐ Spatula

Pan frying means cooking the fish in pre-heated oil in a pan on the stove top. Unlike deep frying where the fish is completely immersed, the oil should hit about half of the fish's height. In pan frying, the fish touches the bottom of the pan, thus giving it a darker color than in deep frying.

After the oil reaches 375°F, place the fish in the pan, then cook until the first side is browned. Flip it immediately, then cook until the second side browns. The second side requires less time since the food is hotter when flipping it than when you started.

Later batches of food will also brown sooner due to the degradation of the oil. Although the batches may turn brown sooner, it doesn't mean they're cooked sooner. Adjust accordingly, strain out errant food particles between batches and add fresh oil if necessary, making sure that you allow the oil to reach 375°F again before adding the fish.

SPICY WHITEFISH ROUNDS

Chef Chris Kibit

Yield: About 24 balls
Prep Time: 45 minutes
Cook Time: 10 minutes

INGREDIENTS

☐ 1 pound fresh Great Lakes whitefish
☐ 1 teaspoon grated fresh ginger
☐ 1 teaspoon salt
☐ 4 scallions, finely chopped
☐ 1½ teaspoons curry powder
☐ 3 eggs
☐ 1 cup fine, dry bread crumbs
☐ 3 tablespoons sesame seeds
☐ Vegetable oil for deep frying
☐ Lemon slices

Preparation

1. Poach or steam fish until just cooked (See Poaching and Steaming techniques on page 16).
2. Cool and flake fish, discarding any skin and bones.
3. Place fish in a bowl and stir in ginger, salt, scallions and curry powder.
4. Beat 1 egg. Add to fish mixture and mix well.
5. Shape into 24 equal balls about ¾ inch in diameter.
6. In a shallow dish, beat remaining 2 eggs.
7. On a sheet of wax paper, mix breadcrumbs and sesame seeds.
8. Dip fish balls in egg. Then roll in the crumb mixture to coat.
9. In a deep, heavy-gauge saucepan heat about 2 inches of oil to 375°F.
10. Add fish balls a few at a time and cook until golden on all sides.
11. Drain on absorbent paper.
12. Serve hot or warm with lemon slices.

Note: You may want to offer your guests a dipping sauce or two, perhaps a sweet one, a spicy one and/ or a soy-based one. I have also successfully used lake trout and salmon with this recipe.

BLACK PEPPER AND SEA SALT WHITEFISH AND CHIPS
With Lemon-Tarragon Aioli

Chef Nathan Mileski

Yield: 4 servings
Prep Time: 30 minutes
Cook Time: 15 minutes

INGREDIENTS

- ☐ 4 large boiling potatoes
- ☐ 12 cups vegetable oil
- ☐ 2 cups all-purpose flour
- ☐ 1 bottle cold beer (preferably ale)
- ☐ 1½ teaspoons Creole seasoning
  (see recipe on page 5)
- ☐ 1½ pounds Great Lakes whitefish fillets,
  skinned, pin-boned and cut diagonally into
  1-inch-wide strips (5–6 inches long)
- ☐ Black pepper to taste
- ☐ Sea salt to taste

Preparation

1. Cut potatoes lengthwise into ½-inch-thick wedges, transferring as cut to a large bowl of ice water.
2. Chill potatoes for 30 minutes.
3. Heat oil in a deep, 6-quart heavy pot over moderately high heat until it registers 325°F on thermometer.
4. While oil is heating, drain potatoes and dry thoroughly with paper towels.
5. Fry ⅓ of potatoes, stirring gently, until edges are just golden, about 4 minutes.
6. Transfer with a slotted spoon to fresh paper towels to drain.
7. Fry remaining potatoes in 2 batches as in steps 5 and 6, returning oil to 325°F between batches.
8. Remove oil from heat and and set aside.
9. Cool potatoes, about 25 minutes.
10. Heat oil over moderately high heat until it registers 350°F.
11. Put oven racks in upper and lower thirds of oven and preheat oven to 250°F.

12. Fry potatoes again, in 3 batches, until deep golden brown and crisp, about 5 minutes per batch. Allow oil to return to 350°F between batches.
13. Transfer with slotted spoon to fresh paper towels as fried and drain briefly, then arrange in one layer in a shallow baking pan. Keep warm in upper third of oven.
14. Increase oil temperature to 375°F.
15. Sift 1½ cups flour into a bowl, then whisk in beer gently until just combined.
16. Stir in ¼ teaspoon salt, ½ teaspoon of coarsely ground black pepper, and Creole seasoning.
17. Pat fish dry.
18. Sprinkle fish on both sides with ¾ teaspoon salt and ¼ teaspoon pepper, then dredge in remaining ½ cup flour, shaking off excess.
19. Coat 4 pieces of fish in batter, 1 at a time, and slide into oil.
20. Fry coated fish, turning over frequently, until deep golden and cooked through, 4–5 minutes.
21. Transfer to a paper-towel-lined baking sheet and keep warm in lower third of oven.
22. Then fry remaining fish in batches of 4, returning oil to 375°F between batches.
23. Give the fish and chips a final seasoning with black pepper and sea salt.
24. Serve with Lemon-Tarragon Aioli.

INGREDIENTS FOR LEMON-TARRAGON AIOLI

- ☐ 1 cup mayonnaise
- ☐ 4 tablespoons chopped fresh tarragon
- ☐ ½ tablespoon chopped fresh garlic
- ☐ ½ tablespoon malt vinegar (Apple cider vinegar may be substituted, but the result will be sweeter.)
- ☐ 1 tablespoon fresh lemon juice

Preparation

1. Combine all ingredients in a bowl, and whisk until incorporated.
2. Chill for at least 30 minutes prior to serving.

INGREDIENTS FOR CREOLE SEASONING

- ☐ 2½ tablespoons paprika
- ☐ 2 tablespoons salt
- ☐ 2 tablespoons garlic powder
- ☐ 1 tablespoon black pepper
- ☐ 1 tablespoon onion powder
- ☐ 1 tablespoon cayenne pepper
- ☐ 1 tablespoon dried leaf oregano

Preparation

1. Mix all ingredients thoroughly.
2. Store away from moisture.

Note: Great as a seasoning for grilled, pan-seared, or broiled whitefish.

POTATO-ENCRUSTED WHITEFISH

Chef Cynthia Manning

Yield: 6 servings
Prep Time: 15–20 minutes
Cook Time: 10–12 minutes

INGREDIENTS

- ☐ ½ pound frozen hash brown potatoes, thawed
- ☐ ¾ teaspoon seasoned salt
- ☐ ½ teaspoon dried dill weed
- ☐ ¼ teaspoon black pepper
- ☐ 6 fresh Great Lakes whitefish fillets (4-ounce portions)
- ☐ ½ teaspoon kosher salt
- ☐ ¼ cup flour
- ☐ 1 egg, beaten with a fork
- ☐ 1 tablespoon butter
- ☐ 2 tablespoons olive oil

Preparation

1. In a bowl, mix thawed hash browns with seasoned salt and pepper.
2. Sprinkle whitefish fillets with salt.
3. Dip flesh side of fish in flour, then egg and place dipped-side up on sheet tray.
4. Sprinkle the hash browns over fillets evenly, using all of them, and pressing them firmly into the fish flesh.
5. Heat half of olive oil and butter in large, non-stick fry pan.
6. Cook half of the fillets, potato-side down first for about 3 minutes per side until potatoes are browned and fish is partially cooked.
7. Carefully flip fillets over and cook another 3 minutes or so until cooked through, being careful not to overcook.
8. Repeat with remaining butter, oil and fillets. Serve hot.

CRISPY TERIYAKI WHITEFISH

Yield: 8 servings
Prep Time: 25 minutes
Cook Time: 20 minutes

INGREDIENTS

- ☐ 8 Great Lakes whitefish fillets (6 ounces each), skinned and pin-boned
- ☐ ½ cup teriyaki sauce
- ☐ 1 cup stir fry sauce
- ☐ Juice of one fresh lemon
- ☐ 2 cups dry potato flakes
- ☐ ½ cup all-purpose flour
- ☐ 2 tablespoons ancho chili seasoning
- ☐ 1 tablespoon garlic powder
- ☐ 1 tablespoon ground black pepper
- ☐ Oil for deep frying

Preparation

1. Mix the teriyaki sauce, stir fry sauce and lemon juice in a shallow bowl.
2. Place the whitefish fillets in the mixture and let sit 15–20 minutes.
3. Heat the oil in a heavy gauge pan to 360°F.
4. Mix the dry ingredients in a shallow bowl.
5. Coat each fillet evenly with the dry mixture.
6. Deep fry the whitefish, 1 or 2 fillets at a time, until golden brown and easily flaked with a fork, about 5 minutes.
7. Serve immediately.

CLASSIC SCANDINAVIAN FISH CAKES

Yield: Makes about 12 cakes or 24 smaller cakes for appetizers
Prep Time: 1 hour
Cook Time: 15 minutes

INGREDIENTS

- ☐ 3 cups steamed or baked Great Lakes whitefish, flaked
- ☐ ½ cup mashed potatoes
- ☐ 1½ tablespoons grated or chopped onion
- ☐ 1 teaspoon finely chopped celery
- ☐ 1 teaspoon chopped fresh parsley
- ☐ 1 teaspoon chopped or dried chives
- ☐ 1 egg, lightly beaten
- ☐ Tomato sauce as needed (about 6–8 ounces)

Preparation

1. Salt and pepper fish to taste.
2. Mix all ingredients together and add just enough tomato sauce to make the mixture moist.
3. Shape mixture into 2½ inch rounds or squares, ½ inch thick.
4. Sprinkle with paprika and pan fry slowly in butter until golden brown. Turn over. Fry slowly so cakes will set and not break apart when turning.
5. Drain briefly on absorbent paper.
6. Serve hot.

FRIED WHITEFISH TACOS

Chef Nathan Mileski

Yield: 4–6 servings
Prep Time: 35 minutes, including accompaniments
Cook Time: 20 minutes

INGREDIENTS

- ☐ 4 cups vegetable oil
- ☐ 12–16 corn tortillas
- ☐ 1 cup all-purpose flour
- ☐ 2 teaspoons salt
- ☐ 1 cup beer (not dark)
- ☐ 1 pound Great Lakes whitefish fillets, cut into 3-inch by 1-inch strips

Preparation

1. Preheat oven to 350°F.
2. Heat 1 inch of oil in a 10-inch heavy pot (2–3 inches deep) over moderate heat until a deep-fat thermometer registers 360°F.
3. Meanwhile, separate tortillas and make 2 stacks of 6–8. Wrap each stack in foil and heat in oven 12–15 minutes.
4. While tortillas are warming, stir together flour and salt in a large bowl.
5. Stir in beer (batter will be thick).
6. Gently stir fish into batter to coat.
7. Lift each piece of fish out of batter, wiping any excess off on side of bowl.
8. Fry fish in batches, turning once or twice, until golden, 4–5 minutes.
9. Increase oil temperature to 375°F and refry fish in batches, turning once or twice, until golden brown and crisp, about 1 minute.
10. Drain on paper towels.
11. Assemble tacos with warm tortillas, fish, and accompaniments.

Accompaniments

- ☐ shredded lettuce or cabbage
- ☐ sour cream
- ☐ avocado slices
- ☐ chopped or sliced radish
- ☐ red or green salsa
- ☐ sliced, pickled jalapeños
- ☐ lime wedges
- ☐ cilantro
- ☐ diced onions

SESAME-CRUSTED WHITEFISH

Yield: 4 servings
Prep Time: 20 minutes
Cook Time: 20 minutes (for several batches)

INGREDIENTS

- ☐ 1½ pounds Great Lakes whitefish, skinned, pin-boned and cut into nuggets
- ☐ 1 tablespoon light soy sauce
- ☐ 1 tablespoon sesame oil
- ☐ 1 cup all-purpose flour for dredging
- ☐ 2 egg whites, beaten
- ☐ 4 tablespoons white sesame seeds
- ☐ 4 tablespoons black sesame seeds
- ☐ Oil for deep frying

Preparation

1. Marinate fish nuggets in soy sauce and sesame oil for 15–20 minutes.
2. Mix black and white sesame seeds together.
3. Drain the fish and dredge in flour.
4. Dip the fish in the egg and then roll it in the sesame seeds.
5. Deep fry the pieces in 360°F oil for 4–5 minutes, but no longer or the seeds will scorch and the fish will overcook.
6. It is advisable to cook the fish in small batches so the oil temperature will not fluctuate too drastically.
7. Keep the cooked fish warm on absorbent paper in a warm oven.

Note: Serve with soy sauce or soy-wasabi mix for a spicier touch.

CHAPTER TWO
SAUTÉING AND STIR FRYING

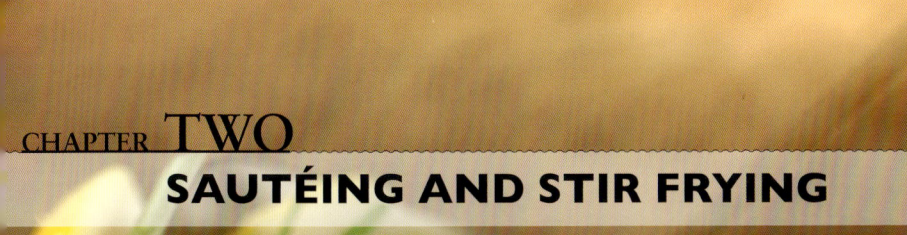

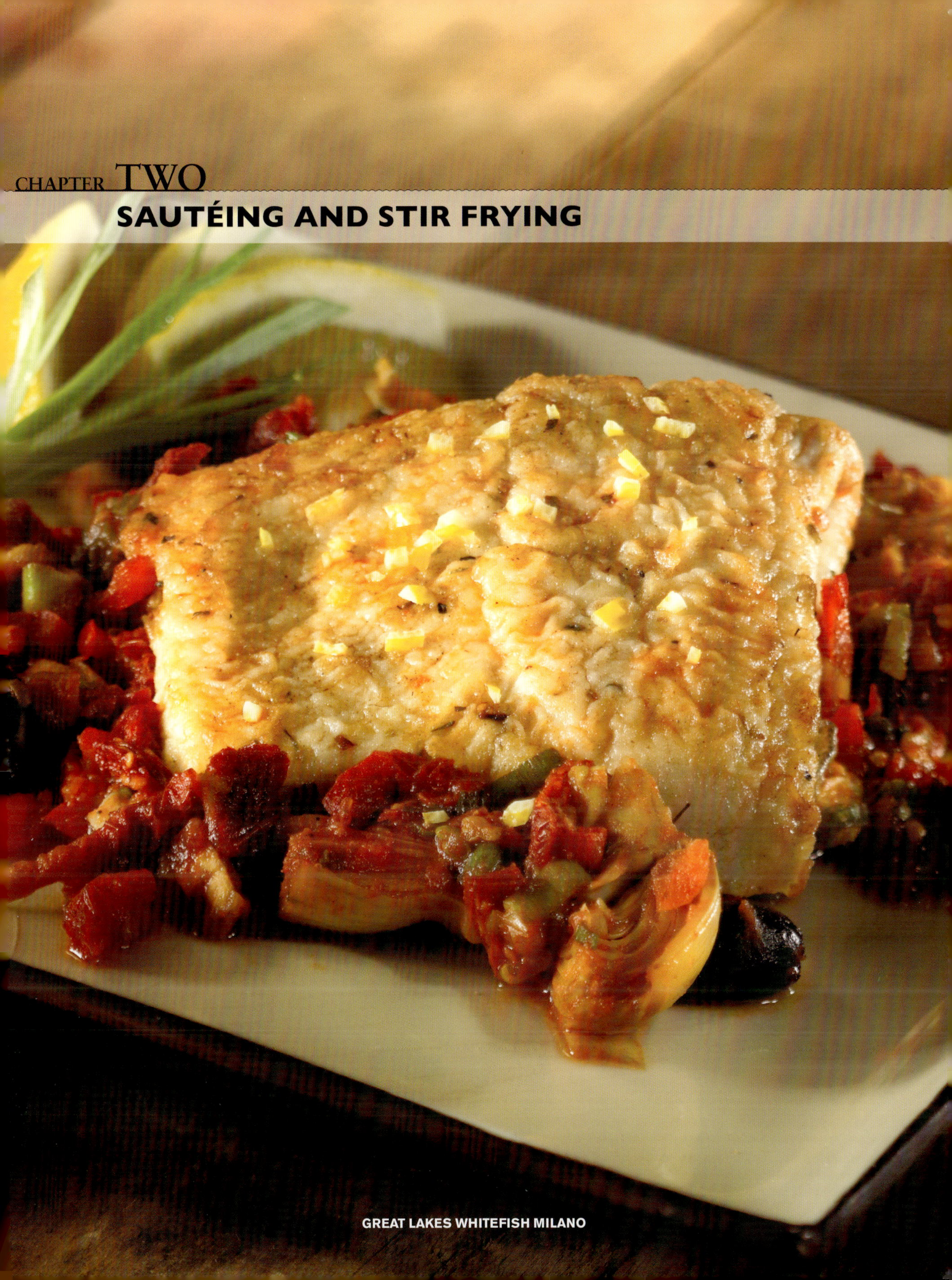

GREAT LAKES WHITEFISH MILANO

Sautéing and Stir Frying Techniques

Equipment

- ☐ Sauté pan or skillet
- ☐ Wok with wok stand or wok skillet
- ☐ Tongs or two spoons for stirring

Sautéing and stir frying are fairly similar styles of cooking. What sets them apart is the type of pan used – a slope-sided sauté pan for sautéing and a deeper slope-sided, round-bottom wok for stir frying. Sautéing and stir frying are both ideal means for searing or browning fish, a process that imparts wonderful flavor. Both are very quick cooking techniques.

Sautéing and stir frying involve cooking small pieces of fish in a small amount of oil or butter over high heat. A sauté pan or a wok made of heavy-gauge stainless steel (with aluminum layered in-between) is ideal. Such a pan will distribute heat evenly without burning your fish and will respond quickly to temperature changes.

It is important not to add the fish to the pan until both the pan and oil or butter are hot. This can be tested by putting a little piece of fish in the pan, and, if it begins to sizzle immediately, the fat is ready. It is also important not to overcrowd the pan because that lowers the temperature too much. When that happens, the food begins to simmer in its own juices, and you can lose that wonderful crisp, browning effect.

Because the fish is cooked over high heat, it must be stirred or moved constantly to prevent burning or sticking, while being gentle so as not to break up the pieces.

Fish fillets can be accented with fresh herbs, or coated with seasoned flour (called dredging) or bread crumbs, before sautéing. See the Pan Frying method to read more about breading.

BLACKENED WHITEFISH

Gauthier & Spaulding Fisheries

Yield: 6 servings
Prep Time: 15 minutes
Cook Time: About 10 minutes

INGREDIENTS

- ☐ 2 tablespoons paprika
- ☐ 1 tablespoon salt
- ☐ 2 teaspoons onion
- ☐ 2 teaspoons garlic powder
- ☐ 2 teaspoons cayenne pepper
- ☐ 2 teaspoons black pepper
- ☐ 2 teaspoons white pepper
- ☐ 1 teaspoon oregano
- ☐ 1 teaspoon thyme
- ☐ 16 tablespoons butter, melted
- ☐ 6 Great Lakes whitefish fillets (6–8 ounces each)

Preparation

1. Heat large cast-iron skillet over high heat for about 10 minutes.
2. Meanwhile, in a medium bowl combine paprika, salt, onion, garlic powder, cayenne, peppers, oregano and thyme; mix thoroughly and set aside.
3. Dip each fillet in melted butter, then season with spice mixture.
4. Place in hot skillet, allowing enough space to flip the fillet.
5. Cook for about 5 minutes.
6. Drizzle more butter and spice on fish and flip.
7. Cook additional 5 minutes, until fish is opaque in center.
8. Serve immediately.

SAUTÉED GREAT LAKES WHITEFISH LIVERS MARSALA

Chef Chris Kibit

A crowd-pleasing appetizer.

Yield: 6 servings
Prep Time: 15 minutes
Cook Time: 10 minutes

INGREDIENTS

- ☐ 1 pound whitefish livers
- ☐ 1½ cups all-purpose flour, seasoned with salt and pepper
- ☐ ½ cup julienned onion
- ☐ ¾ cup bacon, cooked and crumbled
- ☐ 6 tablespoons butter, melted
- ☐ ⅓ cup Marsala wine

Preparation

1. Dredge the livers in the seasoned flour.
2. Heat the butter in a sauté pan.
3. Add the livers after lightly shaking off the excess flour.
4. Turn and cook until they are nearly cooked through (they will firm up), about 2 minutes per side.
5. Add the onions and bacon, and cook until onions are transparent, about 3 minutes.
6. Add the Marsala. Stir carefully.
7. Add the livers back to the pan and simmer for 1 minute.

SAUTÉED WHITEFISH WITH WILD MUSHROOM ALMOND CREAM SAUCE

Your would never guess how simple it is to make this elegant dish. Use a good white wine in the preparation and make sure you have enough to serve with the finished dinner. The fish can be served with risotto and fresh market vegetables.

Yield: 2 servings
Prep Time: 15 minutes
Cook Time: 15–20 minutes

INGREDIENTS

- ☐ 2 Great Lakes whitefish fillets (6–8 ounces each)
- ☐ 1 cup heavy cream
- ☐ 4 tablespoons unsalted butter, divided
- ☐ Salt and white pepper to taste
- ☐ 2 tablespoons sliced almonds
- ☐ All-purpose flour for dredging
- ☐ ¼ cup dry white wine
- ☐ 1 cup sliced morel, chanterelle or other wild mushrooms

Preparation

1. In heavy-bottom skillet, melt half the butter over medium-high heat.
2. Add sliced mushrooms and sauté until golden, about 5 minutes.
3. Add sliced almonds and sauté 1 minute.
4. Add white wine and simmer until liquid reduces to a glaze.
5. Add cream; simmer until sauce thickens, stirring occasionally, about 7 minutes.
6. Season to taste with salt and pepper.
7. Melt remaining butter in another heavy skillet over medium-high heat.
8. Season fillets with salt and pepper, coat lightly with flour.
9. Place fillets in skillet and sauté until just cooked through, about 2 minutes per side.
10. Spoon sauce over fillets and serve.

WHITEFISH MEUNIERE

Despite its fancy sounding name, meuniere (pronounced moon-a-year) is both a sauce and a method of preparation. The word means "miller's wife," thus to cook something meuniere is to cook it by first dredging it in flour. A meuniere sauce is a simple, rustic preparation — brown butter, chopped parsley and lemon.

Yield: 10 servings
Prep Time: 15 minutes
Cook Time: 10 minutes

INGREDIENTS

- ☐ 10 Great Lakes whitefish fillets (6–8 ounces each)
- ☐ 1 teaspoon salt
- ☐ 1 teaspoon pepper
- ☐ 1 cup all-purpose flour
- ☐ 12 tablespoons butter, melted
- ☐ 6 tablespoons dry white wine
- ☐ ¼ cup chopped parsley
- ☐ 10 lemon wedges

Preparation

1. Have all ingredients ready before starting to cook.
2. Heat butter in sauté pan over medium-high heat.
3. Dredge (lightly coat) fish with the flour seasoned with salt and pepper. Shake off excess and place in hot fat, skin-side up.
4. Fish can be cooked in several sauté pans or in batches in the same pan.
5. Sauté until lightly browned. Turn over with a spatula and repeat. Be careful not to break the fillets when turning.
6. Remove the fish from the pan and place on a warm dinner plate, or keep warm on a tray in a warm oven.
7. Deglaze the hot pan by carefully pouring in the wine and lemon juice. Keep the pan away from the stove flame, if using gas. Scrape up the brown bits from the pan to help flavor the sauce.
8. Place the fish back in the pan, skin-side up, and cook for 1 additional minute.

Note: Plate the fish skin-side down and pour any sauce over. Garnish with the chopped parsley and serve with lemon wedge.

SEARED WHITEFISH WITH LEMON RÉMOULADE AND GERMAN FINGERLING POTATO SALAD

Chef Jack J. Delby

Rémoulade: a popular condiment similar to mayonnaise or tartar sauce. It was developed in France and is popular around the world.

Yield: 8 servings
Prep Time: 45 minutes – all items
Cook Time: 15 minutes

INGREDIENTS FOR THE WHITEFISH

- ☐ 8 Great Lakes skin-on whitefish fillets (4 ounces each)
- ☐ 1 tablespoon olive oil
- ☐ Kosher salt and fresh ground pepper to taste

Preparation

1. Season whitefish with salt and pepper, and sear on both sides in oil in a very hot, heavy-bottom sauté pan.
2. Finish in oven, briefly, so as to not overcook the fish (approximately 5 minutes in a 450°F oven).

INGREDIENTS FOR THE LEMON RÉMOULADE

- ☐ 1 egg yolk
- ☐ 1 cup salad oil (or other neutral-tasting oil)
- ☐ ½ teaspoon dry mustard
- ☐ 1 dash hot pepper sauce
- ☐ 1 dash Worcestershire sauce
- ☐ 2 tablespoons lemon juice
- ☐ Salt and pepper to taste
- ☐ 2 tablespoons chopped parsley
- ☐ 2 tablespoons chopped capers

Preparation

1. Put egg yolk, mustard, lemon juice, hot pepper and Worcestershire sauces in a blender or food processor. Turn on high speed and slowly add all of the oil.
2. Add remaining ingredients and set aside.

INGREDIENTS FOR THE GERMAN POTATO SALAD

- ☐ 1½ pounds mixed mini potatoes (Russian Fingerling, Mini New Potato, and/or Mini Purple Peruvian)
- ☐ ½ pound smoked bacon, cooked and julienned; reserve rendered fat
- ☐ ½ cup finely diced onion
- ☐ ⅓ cup sherry vinegar
- ☐ ¼ cup olive oil
- ☐ 1 tablespoon sugar
- ☐ 3 tablespoons chopped fresh dill

Preparation

1. Preheat oven to 350°F.
2. Halve all potatoes and boil in salted water until three-quarters of the way cooked.
3. Toss with onion, oil, bacon, bacon fat, vinegar, sugar, salt and pepper.
4. Spread on a sheet tray and finish in a 350°F oven for 10 minutes.
5. Toss with fresh dill.

To Finish

Assemble with a little more than ¼ pound of the potato salad on the bottom. Place fish on top, at a slight angle and creatively drizzle rémoulade on top. Garnish with more chopped dill or chives.

GREAT LAKES WHITEFISH MILANO

Chef Robin Holmes

Yield: 2 servings
Prep Time: 25 minutes
Cook Time: 15–20 minutes

INGREDIENTS

- ☐ 2 Great Lakes whitefish fillets (6–8 ounces each)
- ☐ 1 cup flour, seasoned with salt, pepper and oregano
- ☐ 2 tablespoons olive oil
- ☐ ¼ cup chopped green onion
- ☐ ¼ cup chopped red bell pepper
- ☐ 8 Kalamata olives, pitted
- ☐ 4 canned artichoke hearts, cut in half
- ☐ 1 tablespoon chopped garlic
- ☐ ¼ cup diced sun-dried tomatoes
- ☐ 1 cup marinara sauce
- ☐ 1 cup white wine
- ☐ 1 tablespoon lemon zest, yellow part only
- ☐ Salt and pepper to taste

Preparation

1. Dip whitefish fillet (skin-side up) in seasoned flour. Do not get flour on skinned side.
2. Fold fish in half, tail to head with the skin side inside the fold.
3. Heat olive oil in a 12-inch skillet.
4. Add folded whitefish, browning each side.
5. Add green onions, bell peppers, Kalamata olives, artichoke hearts, garlic and sun-dried tomatoes. Sauté for 1 minute.
6. Add marinara sauce and cook for 1 minute.
7. Add white wine, mixing with rest of ingredients.
8. Turn fish over and simmer another 2 minutes.
9. Remove fish from pan, leaving sauce. Stir in lemon zest.
10. Portion equal amounts of artichoke, olives and sauce over each fish.

WHITEFISH SALTIMBOCCA

Chef Dale Beaubien

Yield: 2 servings
Prep Time: 20 minutes
Cook Time: 10–12 minutes

INGREDIENTS

- ☐ 4 pieces of Great Lakes whitefish fillets (4 ounces each)
- ☐ 4 long, thin slices of Prosciutto or Serrano Ham
- ☐ 8 sage leaves
- ☐ ½ cup Marsala wine
- ☐ 6 tablespoons butter, divided
- ☐ Salt and white pepper to taste

Preparation

1. Preheat oven to 250°F.
2. Pat fish dry with a paper towel.
3. Place two leaves of sage on each fillet and sprinkle them with salt and pepper.
4. Wrap the ham around the fish, pulling it tight so it covers the sage leaves.
5. In a large sauté pan, melt half the butter over medium-high heat until it foams.
6. After the butter has finished foaming, place the fish pieces in the pan. Throw a pinch of salt in the butter to keep it from scorching and adjust the heat.
7. With all the fish in the pan, baste the fish by spooning the butter over each piece as it cooks.
8. Brown the fish pieces on 1 side, then carefully turn them over and brown the second side.
9. Once cooked, remove the fish from the pan and place on a platter in the oven to stay warm while you make the sauce.
10. Pour off any extra fat from the sauté pan and return it to the heat.
11. Once the pan is hot, add the Marsala and scrape up all the bits from the pan with a wooden spoon. Reduce the liquid down to a third the original volume.
12. Add the rest of the butter and whisk the sauce until it thickens.
13. Remove the pan from the heat.
14. Spoon sauce over fish and serve immediately.

CHAPTER THREE

STEAMING, POACHING AND SOUP-MAKING

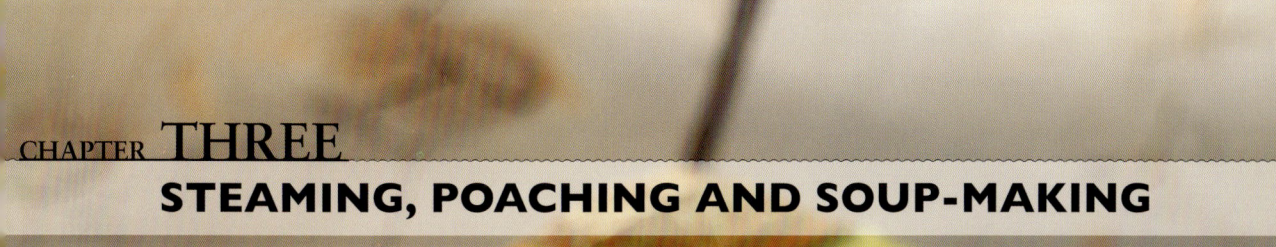

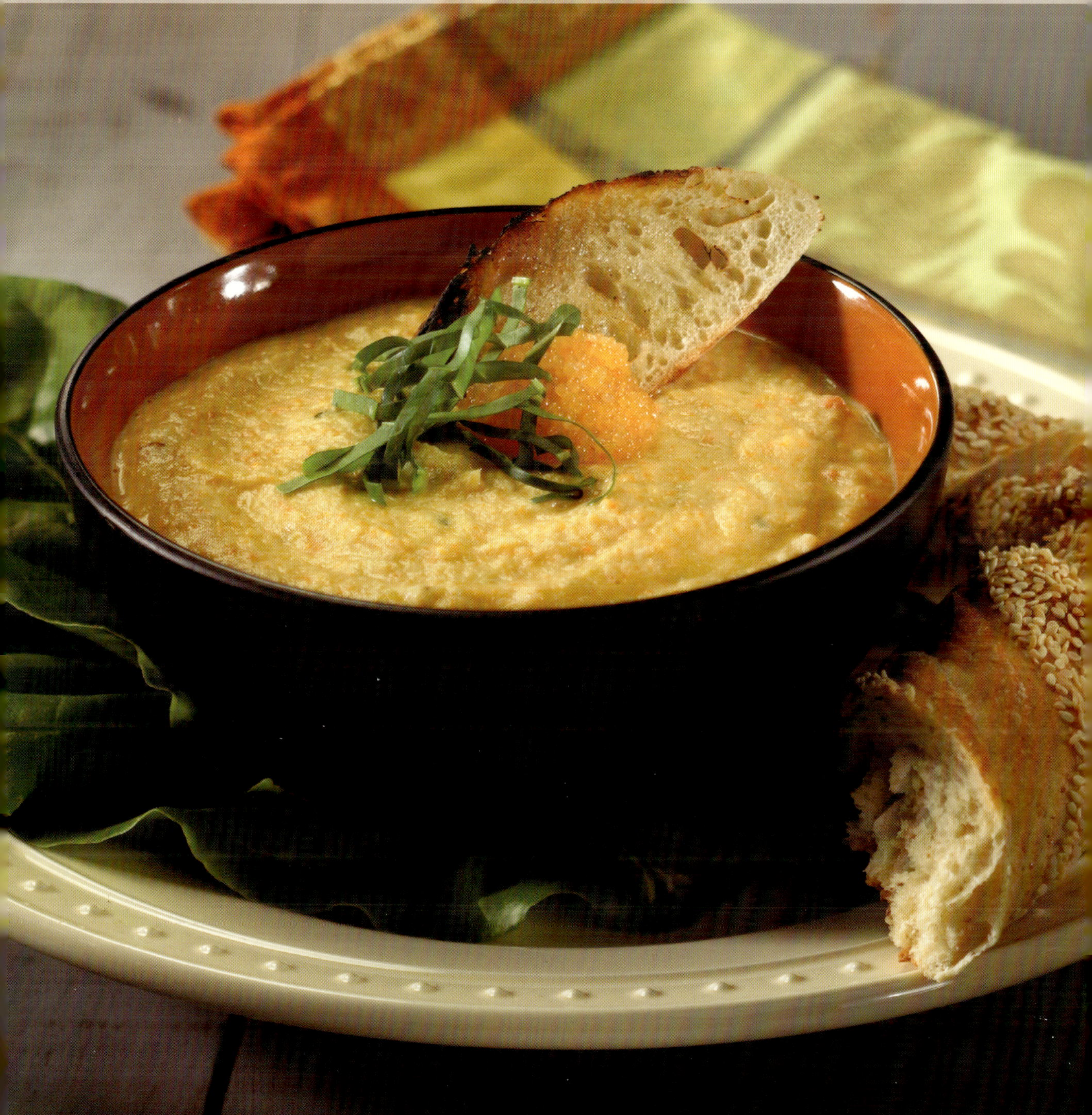

MACKINAC WHITEFISH BISQUE

Steaming, Poaching and Soup-making Techniques

These cooking methods are considered the healthiest of fish cooking techniques because they do not require the use of fats. The liquids used can be water, stock, wine, fruit and vegetable juices or a combination. Usually herbs and spices are added to enhance the flavor. A court bouillon is the most commonly used poaching liquid (see recipe on page 17). When using an acidic liquid such as vinegar or citrus, be sure to use a non-reactive pan such as stainless steel, glass or porcelain. These cooking methods are equally good for either lean or oily fish. People interested in limiting the amount of fat in their diet should consider these cooking methods.

STEAMING

Equipment

☐ Roasting pans, woks, electric frying pans or saucepans can be used with the addition of a steamer basket or rack that elevates the fish above the liquid.
☐ Bamboo steamer
☐ Large spatula for removing fish from rack

Steaming is a moist-heat method of cooking on a rack or steaming basket placed above a simmering liquid and covered. It's a technique that maintains the natural texture and flavor of fish better than any other. It is ideal for delicate lake whitefish, which can be damaged by the greater agitation of boiling. Steaming does not leach any of the nutrients from fish.

POACHING

Equipment

☐ Fish poacher that has a rack with handles
☐ Saucepan
☐ Skillet
☐ Large, slotted spatula
☐ Thermometer with clip to hook on side of pan

Poaching is a fast, gentle cooking method in which fish is immersed in liquid, covered or uncovered. Poaching liquid temperature should be about 160°–185°F, with the water showing few or no bubbles. We have included in this chapter a basic fish stock recipe (see page 21) that can be used as the poaching liquid. The two basic types of poaching methods include shallow poaching (where the fish is not totally immersed in the liquid and is covered with parchment paper) and immersion poaching (where the fish is totally immersed). Poaching is an easy way to imbue a variety of flavors into whitefish. The poaching liquid is often used to create a sauce for the fish after cooking.

SOUP-MAKING

Equipment

☐ Dutch oven, deep skillet, stock pot or soup pot
☐ Thermometer with clip to hook on side of pan
☐ Long-handled spoon

Soup-making is a moist-heat method involving cooking below the boiling point, about 185°–205°F. This is considered a simmer. You will know the temperature is right when tiny bubbles rise to the surface. Whitefish soups, gumbos, bouillabaisse, chowders and bisques are included in this category. Care must be taken not to boil the fish, which breaks down the structure of its tissue.

The quality of the finished product is contingent upon the quality of the ingredients in the recipe and the stock or broth used as the base. We have included in this chapter a recipe for basic fish stock (see page 21) used as a base for many soups and stews. Stocks are a great way to use the bones of fish that otherwise would be thrown away. You can also ask your fish monger for fresh bones. If they have any, they will usually supply them free of charge.

GREAT LAKES WHITEFISH COURT BOUILLON

Chef Deborah Pearce

This court bouillon can be used for poaching or steaming seafood, vegetables or chicken. You can get as creative as you care to with adding different herbs and flavorings to this recipe.

Yield: 1 gallon
Prep Time: 15 minutes
Cook Time: 20 minutes

INGREDIENTS

- ☐ 16 cups water
- ☐ ¼ cup dry white wine
- ☐ Juice of one lemon
- ☐ 1 medium onion, thinly sliced
- ☐ 2 stalks celery, thinly sliced
- ☐ ¼ teaspoon crushed black peppercorns
- ☐ 2 teaspoons salt
- ☐ 1 bay leaf
- ☐ 1 sprig fresh thyme (or ½ teaspoon dried thyme)
- ☐ 10–12 parsley stems (save leaves for garnish or other recipes)

Preparation

1. Place all ingredients in a soup pot.
2. Bring to a boil.
3. Simmer for 15–20 minutes.
4. Strain through a fine strainer, cool and save for use.
5. Will keep refrigerated for up to two weeks.

GRANDPA THILL'S WHITEFISH CHOWDER

Ted Thill

The secret to this recipe is the celery salt. Grandpa Thill said, "If you don't have celery salt, do not even make the chowder!" So, add the celery salt to your taste. This would be excellent served in bread bowls.

Yield: 6–8 servings (cup/bowl)
Prep Time: 25 minutes
Cook Time: 20 minutes

INGREDIENTS

- ☐ ½ cup diced carrots
- ☐ ½ cup diced celery
- ☐ ½ cup chopped onion
- ☐ 1 cup cubed potatoes
- ☐ 1 can (10¾ ounces) condensed cream of mushroom soup
- ☐ 1 can (10¾ ounces) condensed cream of celery soup
- ☐ 1 can (12 ounces) evaporated milk
- ☐ 1 pound skinless Great Lakes whitefish fillets, cubed
- ☐ Pepper to taste
- ☐ Celery salt to taste

Preparation

1. Rinse the cubed whitefish under cold water and let it drain.
2. In a 2-quart soup pot, cook the carrots, celery, onion and potatoes, using as little water as possible.
3. When the vegetables are tender (do not drain), add the cans of soup and the evaporated milk.
4. Continue to stir the pot with a spatula and keep stirring until the mixture is almost to the boiling point.
5. Add the whitefish, pepper and celery salt.
6. Continue stirring for another 7–10 minutes or until the fish is cooked. Be sure to keep stirring so the chowder doesn't scorch and stick to the bottom of the pot.

CHARDONNAY-POACHED GREAT LAKES WHITEFISH WITH COUSCOUS

Chef Rajeev Patgaonkar

Yield: 4 servings
Prep Time: 30 minutes
Cook Time: 20 minutes

INGREDIENTS FOR WHITEFISH

- ☐ 4 skinless Great Lakes whitefish fillets (8 ounces each)
- ☐ ½ cup finely julienned daikon radish
- ☐ ½ cup finely julienned carrots
- ☐ ¼ cup finely julienned green pepper
- ☐ ¼ cup julienned red onion
- ☐ 2 tablespoons roughly chopped cilantro
- ☐ ½ teaspoon salt
- ☐ ¼ teaspoon ground black pepper
- ☐ 1 cup chardonnay
- ☐ ¼ cup olive oil

Preparation

1. Heat oven to 400°F.
2. Cut each fish fillet in half lengthwise.
3. Line the fillets up on parchment paper on a sheet tray.
4. Arrange all julienned vegetables on fish fillets.
5. Sprinkle fillets with chopped cilantro, season with salt and pepper, and drizzle with half of olive oil.
6. Roll the fish (making sure all the vegetables are nicely tucked in) and place each roll in a large shallow flat pan sprayed with cooking oil.
7. Drizzle rest of olive oil and white wine over fillets.
8. Oven poach them covered with foil until fish is no longer translucent in center, about 10–15 minutes.
9. Rest the fillets for a few minutes before serving.
10. Reduce the poaching liquid to half and set it aside as a sauce for plating.

INGREDIENTS FOR COUSCOUS

- ☐ 1 large shallot, minced
- ☐ 2 teaspoons olive oil
- ☐ 1 cup Moroccan couscous
- ☐ ½ cup frozen edamame, defrosted
- ☐ 2¼ cups hot water
- ☐ 1 tablespoon unsalted butter
- ☐ Salt and pepper

Preparation for Couscous

1. Heat olive oil in a quart sauce pan. Sauté shallots and edamame for a minute.
2. Add hot water and bring to boil.
3. Add couscous and mix well.
4. Cover and turn heat off.
5. After 5 minutes, add butter and use a fork to loosen the couscous grains.
6. Season couscous with salt and pepper.

INGREDIENTS FOR CILANTRO SAUCE

- ☐ 2 cups packed cilantro, large stems removed
- ☐ ¼ cup unsalted cashew nuts (raw) soaked in cold water for about 30 minutes before use
- ☐ ¼ cup red onion, chopped
- ☐ 2 small cloves garlic
- ☐ ½ teaspoon jalapeño, chopped and seeded
- ☐ ½ teaspoon kosher salt
- ☐ ¼ cup olive oil, divided
- ☐ ¼ cup water
- ☐ ½ cup fresh lime juice

Preparation for Cilantro Sauce

1. In a food processor:
   a. Pulse all the ingredients except oil until well blended.
   b. With the food processor running, slowly add the olive oil in a steady stream.
   c. Check for seasoning and adjust if needed.
2. Refrigerate until using. Add more oil as needed for your use. Makes 1 cup.

Whatever you don't use, freeze for future needs.

INGREDIENTS FOR GARNISH

- ☐ 4 lime wedges
- ☐ 8 springs of cilantro (nice long ones)
- ☐ Cilantro Sauce
- ☐ 12 grape tomatoes, halved

Plating: At the center of a bowl or plate, put a scoop of couscous. Place two pieces of poached stuffed fish atop the couscous. Form a triangle with 6 halves of grape tomatoes. Drizzle fish and plate with Cilantro Sauce. Garnish with two sprigs of cilantro. Serve with a lime wedge on side.

MACKINAC WHITEFISH BISQUE

Chef Hans Burtscher

This Great Lakes whitefish bisque, garnished with tangy smoked Great Lakes trout and caviar, was a hit with chefs at the renowned James Beard House in New York.

Yield: 8 servings
Prep Time: 40 minutes
Cook Time: 35 minutes

INGREDIENTS

- ☐ 1 tablespoon butter
- ☐ ½ cup diced onions
- ☐ ½ cup diced celery root
- ☐ ½ cup diced carrots
- ☐ 1 tablespoon minced garlic
- ☐ 1½ pounds Great Lakes whitefish, cubed
- ☐ 6 cups fish stock or vegetable stock
- ☐ ½ cup white wine
- ☐ 1 cup coconut milk
- ☐ 1 tablespoon chopped ginger
- ☐ 2 tablespoons thyme
- ☐ 2 tablespoons finely diced lemongrass
- ☐ 1 Idaho potato, peeled and diced
- ☐ 2 cups heavy cream
- ☐ 1 cup crème fraiche (optional)
- ☐ Salt and white pepper as needed

Preparation

1. Melt butter in saucepan on low heat.
2. Add onions, celery root, carrots and garlic and sauté for approximately 4–5 minutes.
3. Add whitefish and sauté for additional 3 minutes.
4. Add white wine, fish stock, coconut milk, lemon-grass, thyme, ginger, potatoes, salt and pepper.
5. Bring mixture to a simmer and cook until reduced by half.
6. Remove saucepan from heat and cool slightly.
7. Transfer ingredients to a blender and purée until smooth.
8. Transfer ingredients back into the saucepan and return to a simmer.
9. Stir in cream and adjust seasonings, if needed.
10. Add crème fraiche just before serving.

INGREDIENTS FOR SMOKED TROUT AND FENNEL RAGOUT

- ☐ 1 tablespoon olive oil
- ☐ ⅓ cup diced smoked trout
- ☐ ⅓ cup diced cooked fennel
- ☐ ⅓ cup diced tomato
- ☐ 1 tablespoon garlic
- ☐ 1 tablespoon chopped chives
- ☐ ½ cup pernod (a licorice-flavored liqueur)
- ☐ Salt and pepper as needed

Preparation

1. Heat olive oil in sauté pan on medium heat.
2. Add trout, fennel, tomatoes, garlic, salt, pepper and sauté for 2–3 minutes.
3. Then add pernod and chives; sauté 1 more minute.
4. Remove the ragout from the heat. Use the ragout to garnish the bisque and top with salmon caviar.

STEAMED WHITEFISH IN A BLACK BEAN AND GARLIC SAUCE

Yield: 6 servings
Prep Time: 25 minutes
Cook Time: About 20 minutes

INGREDIENTS

- ☐ 2 whole Great Lakes whitefish (about 3 pounds each)
- ☐ 2 tablespoons fermented black bean paste
- ☐ ½ cup white wine
- ☐ 1 tablespoon soy sauce
- ☐ 2 tablespoons crushed garlic
- ☐ 1 teaspoon crushed ginger
- ☐ 1 teaspoon crushed chili pepper
- ☐ 4 tablespoons plus 2 teaspoons toasted sesame oil, divided
- ☐ Salt and pepper to taste
- ☐ ½ red pepper, diced, for garnish
- ☐ 2 green onions, chopped, for garnish

Preparation

1. If the fish is still intact, remove gills and scales.
2. Wash the inside with cold water, then rub it with about 1 teaspoon salt.
3. Rub the inside and outside with your favorite white wine.
4. Slice the belly of the fish completely from head to tail, allowing the fish to be spread open flat.
5. Remove the spinal cord by slicing along both sides and lifting it out.
6. To prevent the fish from curling while cooking, make deep cuts about every 1–1½ inches crosswise across the outside (skin side), front to back.
7. Mix black bean paste, salt to taste, leftover white wine (should be about 1 tablespoon), soy sauce, garlic, ginger and chili pepper.
8. Add a dash of toasted sesame oil.
9. Spread the sauce over the skin side of the fish and push the sauce into the deep cuts you made.
10. Sprinkle with chopped red pepper. This is optional but it does give some color.
11. Place fish in a steamer and steam until done. It should take about 10 minutes for every inch thickness of the fish at its thickest part.
12. Remove the fish from the steamer and sprinkle it with chopped green onion.
13. Ladle a small amount of very hot toasted sesame oil onto the fish so it sizzles when you splash it on.
14. Serve immediately.

STEWED GREAT LAKES WHITEFISH WITH TOMATOES AND GARLIC

Yield: 4 servings
Prep Time: 25 minutes
Cook Time: 15 minutes

INGREDIENTS

- ☐ 1 large bunch fresh cilantro, chopped
- ☐ 3 cloves of garlic, minced
- ☐ 3 tomatoes, sliced
- ☐ 2 cups thinly sliced fresh greens such as kale or Swiss chard
- ☐ 4 Great Lakes whitefish fillets (5–6 ounces each)
- ☐ ¼ cup olive oil
- ☐ 1 tablespoon Hungarian-style paprika
- ☐ ½ teaspoon cumin
- ☐ ½ teaspoon turmeric
- ☐ ½ teaspoon ground white pepper
- ☐ 3–4 cups chicken broth or fish stock (see recipe on page 21)

Preparation

1. Spread cilantro evenly over the bottom of a Dutch oven.
2. Sprinkle with garlic and arrange greens, then tomatoes over top.
3. Set whitefish on tomatoes.
4. Whisk oil and dry spices in a small bowl and pour over fish.
5. Add enough broth or stock to reach the bottom of the fish.
6. Bring to just under a boil.
7. Cover and reduce heat to low.
8. Simmer until fish is flaky and greens are tender, about 10 minutes.

Note: Serve on top of vegetables with whole grain pilaf or rice.

WHITEFISH CIOPPINO

Great meal on its own served with crusty bread.

Yield: 8 servings
Prep Time: 45 minutes
Cook Time: 1 hour 25 minutes

INGREDIENTS

- ☐ 1 large onion, chopped
- ☐ 1 medium green pepper, chopped
- ☐ ½ cup sliced celery
- ☐ 1 carrot, pared and shredded
- ☐ 3 cloves garlic, minced
- ☐ 3 tablespoons olive oil
- ☐ 2 cans (1 pound each) chopped tomatoes
- ☐ 1 can (8 ounces) tomato sauce
- ☐ 1 teaspoon dried sweet basil
- ☐ 1 bay leaf
- ☐ ¼ teaspoon pepper
- ☐ 1 pound Great Lakes whitefish fillets, pin-boned
- ☐ 1 dozen clams
- ☐ 1½ cups white wine
- ☐ 1 pound shrimp, shelled and deveined
- ☐ ½ pound scallops
- ☐ 2 tablespoons coarsely chopped fresh Italian parsley
- ☐ Salt to taste

Preparation

1. Sauté onion, green pepper, celery, carrot and garlic in olive oil.
2. Stir in tomatoes, tomato sauce, basil, bay leaf, salt and pepper.
3. Heat to almost boiling, then reduce heat.
4. Cover and simmer 1 hour.
5. Cut whitefish into bite-size pieces.
6. Scrub clams.
7. Stir in wine.
8. Add whitefish, shrimp and scallops.
9. Simmer covered for 10 minutes.
10. Place clams in a layer on top of fish.
11. Cover and steam 5–10 minutes or until clams open. Discard any unopened clams.
12. Place even quantities of each seafood into large pasta or soup bowls and pour remaining soup over seafood. Sprinkle with parsley.
13. Serve hot.

BASIC WHITEFISH STOCK

Yield: 1 quart
Prep Time: 15 minutes
Cook Time: 40 minutes

INGREDIENTS

- ☐ 2 pounds fresh Great Lakes whitefish bones
- ☐ 1½ quarts water
- ☐ 1 medium onion, diced
- ☐ 1 small carrot, diced
- ☐ 1 stalk celery, diced
- ☐ ¼ cup sliced mushrooms
- ☐ 1 bay leaf
- ☐ ¼ teaspoon dried thyme
- ☐ 4–6 whole peppercorns, crushed
- ☐ 2 sprigs fresh parsley

Preparation

1. Make a sachet by bundling the bay leaf, thyme, crushed peppercorns and parsley in a bit of cheesecloth, then tying with string.
2. Combine all other ingredients in a large soup pot.
3. Toss in the sachet. This will keep the seasonings from making your stock murky.
4. Bring mixture to a simmer and cook 30–40 minutes.
5. Skim impurities as they rise to the surface and discard.
6. Remove sachet and dispose of it.
7. Strain, cool and refrigerate the stock.
8. Can be frozen and used as needed.

THAI WHITEFISH HOR MOK

Chef Nathan Mileski

Hor mok is an elegant recipe full of rich flavors that represent all of what I love about Thai food. This heavenly combination of fish, red curry paste, Thai kaffir lime leaves, sugar and coconut cream is one of my all-time favorites. Hor Mok may be hard to find in your local Thai restaurant, but if it's on the menu that's a sign that the restaurant is good and also authentic.

To make it in an American kitchen, some simple modifications yield the same fantastic result. The classic cup is made with banana leaves, by overlapping two circle cuts and folding together with toothpicks. I have modified the classic recipe to use bell peppers as the "cups," as banana leaves are sometimes hard to find in Michigan's Upper Peninsula. Always steam hor mok; a stacked or bamboo steamer works perfectly.

Yield: 4 servings
Prep Time: 25 minutes
Cook Time: 20 minutes

INGREDIENTS

- ☐ 5 or 6 bell peppers (red and green), tops cut off to form cups
- ☐ 2 cups of bite-sized chunks of Great Lakes whitefish
- ☐ 1 tablespoon red curry paste
- ☐ ¾ cup coconut cream
- ☐ 2 tablespoons fish sauce
- ☐ 1½ tablespoons sugar
- ☐ 1 egg
- ☐ 3–5 fresh Thai kaffir lime leaves, finely sliced, or lime zest
- ☐ 2 cups sliced cabbage (preferably Napa cabbage)
- ☐ 1 cup fresh Thai basil leaves to taste
- ☐ Red bell pepper (or red chili peppers), sliced for garnish

Preparation

1. Prepare your cabbage in advance by either steaming it or by putting it in a microwave oven with ½ cup of water, cook for 3 minutes, then let sit to cool.
2. Drain and squeeze the water out of the cabbage. Set aside.
3. Lightly beat the egg.
4. In a medium-sized mixing bowl, put the whitefish, then the red curry paste, followed by the coconut cream, a little at a time.
5. Mix gently until blended together.
6. Add the egg, fish sauce, half of the sugar, and mix well until it thickens.
7. Line the bell peppers with the fresh basil and cabbage.
8. Put the fish mixture into the pepper cups.
9. Top with finely sliced lime leaves, sliced bell peppers, and a few drops of coconut cream.
10. Place the filled peppers into a steamer, and steam for about 20 minutes until the fish is cooked and the sauce has set into a custard-like consistency.

To serve

Garnish each bowl with a teaspoon or so of coconut cream and a slivered fresh Thai chili pepper (optional).

MARQUETTE WHITEFISH CHOWDER

Chef Nathan Mileski

Yield: Makes 2 generous servings
Prep Time: 25 minutes
Cook Time: 20 minutes

INGREDIENTS

- ☐ 4 bacon slices, cut into ½ inch squares
- ☐ 1 tablespoon olive oil
- ☐ ½ cup diced (⅓ inch) onion
- ☐ ¼ cup diced (⅓ inch) green bell pepper
- ☐ ¼ cup diced (⅓ inch) celery
- ☐ 1 tablespoon finely chopped garlic
- ☐ 1 small peeled boiling potato, diced (⅓ inch)
- ☐ 2 bottles (8 ounces each) clam juice
- ☐ 1 tablespoon Asian fish sauce (if handy)
- ☐ 1 can (28 ounces) diced tomatoes, including juice
- ☐ 2 pin-boned, skinless Great Lakes whitefish fillets
  (6–8 ounces each), cut into 1 inch cubes
- ☐ 2 tablespoons chopped fresh flat-leaf parsley
- ☐ Kosher salt to taste
- ☐ Freshly ground black pepper to taste

Preparation

1. Cook bacon with olive oil in a 2- to 3-quart heavy saucepan, stirring over moderate heat until golden, about 5 minutes.
2. Reduce heat to moderately low.
3. Add onion, bell pepper, celery and garlic and cook, stirring until softened, about 5 minutes.
4. Stir in potato, clam juice, fish sauce and tomatoes (with juice) and simmer covered for about 10 minutes.
5. Stir in whitefish and simmer covered. Stir occasionally until whitefish is cooked through, about 5–7 minutes.
6. Remove pan from heat.
7. Stir in parsley, salt and pepper to taste.

NOTES

BROILED WHITEFISH WITH CAPER BERRY AIOLI

Broiling, Grilling and Campfire Cooking Techniques

The techniques in this chapter encompass various ways of cooking lake whitefish with a heat source directly above or below.

BROILING

Equipment

☐ Broiler pan
☐ Long-handled spatula
☐ Long-handled brush for basting
☐ Non-stick vegetable spray

Broiling is a dry, high-heat cooking technique in which the energy source is located directly above the fish. It is a quick, non-greasy method that helps the fish develop a golden surface while the inside cooks. The fish develops its own rich flavor under the intense heat, but can also be complemented by basting or using an accompanying sauce.

Before cooking, make sure your broiler has completely preheated. Lightly brush the fish fillet with butter, oil or an oil-based marinade. This will add flavor, help prevent sticking and facilitate a uniform sear.

Because this technique involves very high heat, it bears watching closely. Your stove's manual may include suggestions for ventilating the oven so that the fish and other food does not burn. Read and follow those instructions carefully.

GRILLING

Equipment

☐ Indoor or outdoor gas or charcoal grill
☐ Fish basket or grill screen
☐ Heavy-duty aluminum foil
☐ Long-handled tongs
☐ Long-handled spatula
☐ Long-handled brush for basting
☐ Non-stick vegetable spray
☐ Charcoal
☐ Charcoal starter
☐ Wire brush

This dry-heat cooking method involves using a heat source below the fish and is best suited to using the whole fish or whole fillets. Place them in an oiled, wire fish basket or grilling screen, because the delicate nature of whitefish does not lend itself to being placed directly on the grill. Aluminum foil can also be used.

FUEL SOURCE

GAS GRILLS – Follow the manufacturer's instructions to prepare the grill for cooking at the appropriate temperature. Also, it's very important to oil the fish grilling basket or grill screen to prevent sticking.

CHARCOAL GRILLS - Although gas grills are convenient, some people prefer grilling with charcoal as the fuel source.

The most commonly used charcoal is the briquette. The advantage to using briquettes is that you can easily gauge the way they are going to burn, with even, consistent heat for a reasonably long time.

JUDGING THE TEMPERATURE OF THE GRILL

You can judge the temperature of the grill (if you don't have a thermometer) by placing your hand palm-side down just over the grill. Count (using "one-thousand-one, one-thousand-two," and so on), until the heat is uncomfortable. If you can keep your hand in place for 2 seconds, the fire is hot (375°F); if 4 seconds, it is medium (300–350°F); 5 seconds means the fire heat is low (200–300°F).

COOKING WHOLE FISH

When grilling whole fish, ignite the coals about 45 minutes before you plan to begin cooking. You will need 25–50 long-burning briquettes. Wipe the fish with damp cloth, inside the body cavity and out. Sprinkle salt and pepper inside and tuck in lemon, onion and parsley sprigs. Cut one piece of heavy-duty foil which, when doubled, will fit the length of the fish from head to tail and will provide two layers of protection and support.

When coals are completely covered with gray ash, divide them in half and arrange one half in a long row, 2 briquettes wide and the length of the fish. Arrange the remaining briquettes in the same manner, parallel to the first row, but leaving an empty channel the width of the fish down the center of the grill. This allows the fish to receive indirect heat from coals, rather than direct heat from coals, which could burn the fish's bottom before it cooks on top. Adjust grill height to about 6 inches above the coals. When the coals are moderately hot, place the fish foil side down on the center of the grill, between the rows of coals.

If you have a covered grill, place the lid over it and adjust dampers to maintain high heat. If your grill is uncovered, tear off enough heavy-duty foil to cover the grill completely, and tuck foil over its edges to seal in the heat and smoke.

Allow 10 minutes cooking time per inch thickness of fish, measured at the thickest part. When done, the fish will be firmer and less translucent than raw, and will register about 145°F on a meat thermometer. To serve, lift off the top layer of skin. Cut directly to the bone, slide a wide spatula between the flesh and ribs, and lift off each serving. When the top half has been served, lift and remove the backbone and cut down to the skin to serve the remaining half.

CAMPFIRE COOKING

Equipment

- ☐ Grate
- ☐ Long-handled spatula
- ☐ Long tongs
- ☐ Oven mitt
- ☐ Cooking oil
- ☐ Wooden matches in watertight container
- ☐ Seasoned cast-iron skillet
- ☐ Heavy-duty aluminum foil
- ☐ Firewood or charcoal

Campfire fish cooking is similar to cooking fish over a grill when using a grate, or similar to stovetop cooking when a pan is used. The challenge with campfire cooking rests in the variable heat and the outdoor conditions, so pay extra attention that the fish cooks without becoming too done.

BROILED WHITEFISH WITH LEMON-TARRAGON SAUCE

Yield: 6 Servings
Prep Time: 15 minutes
Cook Time: 6–10 minutes

INGREDIENTS

- ☐ 6 Great Lakes whitefish fillets (8 ounces each), skin on
- ☐ ½ cup bottled clam juice
- ☐ 2 tablespoons fresh lemon juice
- ☐ 1 tablespoon tarragon vinegar
- ☐ 3 tablespoons fresh tarragon leaves
- ☐ ¾ cup plus 2 tablespoons olive oil
- ☐ Dash of hot sauce
- ☐ Salt to taste

Preparation

1. Bring clam juice to a boil in a small, heavy saucepan and reduce to 2 tablespoons, about 5 minutes.
2. Transfer to blender and add fresh lemon juice, vinegar and tarragon leaves.
3. Blend mixture until tarragon is finely chopped.
4. With machine running on lowest setting, gradually add ¾ cup oil until it becomes emulsified.
5. Season to taste with salt and hot sauce.
6. Position the oven rack 6 inches from the broiler. Preheat the broiler.
7. Brush fish with 2 tablespoons oil; season with salt and pepper.
8. Place fish skin-side down on heavy, large baking sheet lined with foil or parchment paper for easy clean up.
9. Broil without turning until opaque in center, about 6 minutes.
10. Transfer whitefish to plates. Spoon sauce over fish and serve.

Note: Garnish with a fresh sprig of tarragon and lemon slices.

GRILLED WHITEFISH WITH DIJON MUSTARD CRUST

Herbs de Provence is a mixture of dried herbs representative of those used in the French region of Provence. The standard mixture typically contains savory, fennel, basil, and thyme flowers and other herbs, including lavender in American mixtures. The proportions vary, but thyme usually dominates the flavor.

Yield: 4 servings
Prep Time: 10 minutes
Cook Time: 10 minutes

INGREDIENTS

- ☐ 4 skinless Great Lakes whitefish fillets (4 ounces each)
- ☐ 4 tablespoons Dijon-style mustard
- ☐ 8 tablespoons dry, unseasoned bread crumbs
- ☐ 1½ tablespoons Herbs de Provence seasoning
- ☐ Salt and pepper to taste
- ☐ 3 tablespoons olive oil

Preparation

1. Preheat a grill to medium heat.
2. Season breadcrumbs with salt, pepper and Herbs de Provence.
3. Coat each fillet with a thick layer of Dijon-style mustard.
4. Dip each fillet in bread crumb mix.
5. Brush grill with the oil and place each fillet on the grill.
6. Grill for approximately 5 minutes, flip and grill other side until done.

Note: Turning the fish on the grill can be a delicate procedure, so make sure you have a spatula large enough to hold the whole fillet or use a well-oiled grill basket.

CEDAR PLANK-ROASTED WHITEFISH WITH ROASTED TOMATO AND OLIVE RELISH

Chef Paul Carlson

Yield: 4 servings
Prep Time: 15 minutes + 1 hour to soak planks
Cook Time: 10 minutes

INGREDIENTS

- ☐ 4 pin-boned Great Lakes whitefish fillets (6–8 ounces each)
- ☐ 1 pint cherry tomatoes
- ☐ 1 tablespoon finely diced shallots
- ☐ 1 tablespoon Verjus* (or substitute champagne vinegar)
- ☐ 2 tablespoons sliced brine-cured olives (such as Kalamata)
- ☐ 1 tablespoon fresh basil
- ☐ 2 tablespoons olive oil
- ☐ Salt and pepper to taste
- ☐ 2–4 cedar planks

Preparation

1. Preheat oven to 400°F.
2. Place cedar planks in water and weigh them down with a heavy plate to ensure they become saturated. (I purchase planks from the local hardware store; just be sure that they have not been chemically treated).
3. Next, lightly coat the tomatoes with olive oil, salt and pepper.
4. Roast tomatoes in oven for 15 minutes, or until they start to burst.
5. Combine tomatoes, shallots, olives, olive oil, Verjus and fresh basil. Set mixture aside at room temperature.
6. Set grill to medium-high and place planks on grill surface.
7. Lightly coat the surface of whitefish with oil, salt and pepper.
8. Place fish on planks and roast until just cooked through, 8–10 minutes.
9. Top with tomato mixture.

Note: Serve fish on a bed of wilted greens such as arugula or spinach.

*Verjus (or "green juice") is the pressing of underripe grapes, a by-product of the winery. Verjus shares the same acid balance as wine and this lends itself nicely to foods being enjoyed with wine. Vinegar, such as champagne vinegar, makes a fine substitute.

WHITEFISH MARINADE

Gauthier & Spaulding Fisheries

Yield: 1 cup
Prep Time: 5 minutes + marinating time

INGREDIENTS

½ cup dry white wine
1 teaspoon dill weed
½ cup lemon juice
3 tablespoons butter, melted

Preparation

1. Prepare marinade by mixing all ingredients together.

When using this marinade, prepare as follows:

1. Using ⅔ of the marinade, marinate fish fillets for 30 minutes.
2. Broil or bake fish (or in foil on grill) for 10–12 minutes, or until fish is opaque and flakes.
3. While broiling, baste fish with reserved marinade.

BROILED WHITEFISH WITH CAPER BERRY AIOLI

Chef Jeffrey Kudrna

Yield: 4 servings
Prep Time: 25 minutes
Cook Time: 10 minutes

INGREDIENTS

- ☐ 4 Great Lakes whitefish fillets (6 ounces each)
- ☐ 5 caper berries or ½ cup of capers
- ☐ 2 medium eggs
- ☐ 2 cups canola oil
- ☐ ¼ fresh lemon
- ☐ 1 teaspoon white wine (optional)
- ☐ Salt and pepper to taste

Preparing the aioli

1. Put 2 eggs and caper berries (or capers) into food processor. Spin until capers are chopped.
2. Drizzle oil in slowly while processor is moving, and it will start to have the consistency of mayonnaise. If it separates, remove from processor, add 2 more eggs and SLOWLY add mixture back in until it thickens.
3. Squeeze fresh lemon juice into aioli while processor is spinning. Add white wine to mixture.
4. Add salt and pepper to taste.

Preparing the whitefish

1. Preheat the oven to 400°F.
2. Run your fingers down the fillet. If you don't feel the pin bones (there are approximately 32 pin bones per fillet) skip this step. If you do feel the pin bones, remove them with pliers.
3. Place fillets on baking pan and bake 12 minutes or until almost done. Fish should separate easily when touched.
4. Take fish out, and spread aioli on fillets in a thick layer.
5. Place under broiler until a light golden brown color, about 2 minutes.

Do not overcook: Aioli will turn into scrambled eggs and will be undesirable.

Note: Serve with your favorite roasted potatoes and seasonal vegetables.

BARBECUED WHITEFISH FILLETS

Gauthier & Spaulding Fisheries

Yield: 6 servings
Prep Time: 30 minutes
Cook Time: 10–16 minutes

INGREDIENTS

- ☐ 2 pounds Great Lakes whitefish fillets, cut into 6 portions
- ☐ ¼ cup chopped onion
- ☐ 2 tablespoons chopped green peppers
- ☐ 1 clove garlic, finely chopped
- ☐ 2 tablespoons melted butter
- ☐ 2 teaspoons salt
- ☐ 1 can (8 ounces) tomato sauce
- ☐ 2 tablespoons lemon juice
- ☐ 1 tablespoon Worcestershire sauce
- ☐ 1 tablespoon sugar
- ☐ ¼ teaspoon pepper

Preparation

1. Cook onion, green pepper and garlic in butter until tender.
2. Add remaining ingredients and simmer for 5 minutes, stirring occasionally. Cool.
3. Place fish in a single layer in a shallow baking dish. Pour most of the sauce over the fish (retaining some for basting) and let stand for 30 minutes, turning once.
4. Remove fish and place onto a well-greased, hinged, wire grill.
5. Cook about 4 inches from moderately hot coals for 5–8 minutes, basting with sauce.
6. Turn and cook for an additional 5–8 minutes, continuing to baste, until fish flakes easily when tested with a fork.

WHITEFISH IN FOIL ALA VERACRUZANA

Chef Robin Holmes

Yield: 4 servings
Prep Time: 25 minutes
Cook Time: 20 minutes

INGREDIENTS

- ☐ 4 Great Lakes whitefish fillets (8 ounces each)
- ☐ Juice of 1 lemon
- ☐ Salt and pepper to taste
- ☐ 1 tablespoon olive oil
- ☐ 1 small onion, sliced into thin strips
- ☐ 2 cloves garlic, minced
- ☐ 1 jalapeño pepper, seeded and sliced
- ☐ ½ cup chopped red bell peppers
- ☐ 1½ pounds fresh tomatoes, peeled, seeded and chopped
- ☐ ¼ cup capers
- ☐ ½ cup green olives
- ☐ ½ cup chopped green onion
- ☐ ½ cup sliced almonds, toasted
- ☐ ½ cup fresh minced cilantro
- ☐ 1 lime, quartered

Preparation

1. Preheat oven to 400°F.
2. Sprinkle fish with lemon juice, salt and pepper. Set aside while preparing sauce.
3. In heavy-bottom sauté pan, heat olive oil, add onion, garlic, jalapeño and bell peppers. Sauté over medium heat until soft.
4. Add tomatoes, capers, green olives, and simmer 15–20 minutes. Add salt and pepper to taste.
5. Cut 4 rectangles of aluminum foil, large enough to accommodate the fish fillets.
6. Brush foil with olive oil and lay one fillet on each piece.
7. Spoon 2 heaping tablespoons of sauce on each fillet.
8. Loosely fold the foil over the fish, and crimp the edges together.
9. Place fish packets on baking sheet and cook in preheated oven 15–20 minutes.
10. To serve, carefully cut into top of foil and pull apart. Sprinkle with fresh green onion, toasted almonds and fresh cilantro. Serve with lime wedge.

NOTES

PISTACHIO-CRUSTED GREAT LAKES WHITEFISH WITH CITRUS SPINACH SALAD

Roasting and Baking Techniques

The terms roasting and baking are often used interchangeably, but there are some useful distinctions. Roasting is usually done at higher temperatures (375°–400°F) for a shorter period of time, while baking is at lower temperatures (325°–350°F) for a bit longer. These methods lend themselves to a wide variety of flavor profiles and creativity. The primary concern when baking or roasting lean whitefish is to maintain moisture. The recipes in this chapter will help you do so. Below are some of the different types of oven cooking that can be done with fish. Allow about 10 minutes of cooking for each inch of thickness measured at the thickest part of the fish.

Equipment

- ☐ Baking pan or roasting pan
- ☐ Large spatula (for handling whole fish)
- ☐ Glass baking dishes
- ☐ Baking sheet (cookie sheet with sides)

- ☐ Cast-iron skillet
- ☐ Casserole dish
- ☐ Baster or basting brush
- ☐ Parchment paper or aluminum foil

IN PARCHMENT

(En Papillote – from French meaning wrapped in parchment paper)

This technique consists of oven-baking the fish in sealed parchment or aluminum foil. This can be done with or without stuffing, sometimes with other flavors such as fresh herbs or citrus. The packet allows the fish to cook in its own juice to preserve moistness, nutrients and flavor. This method is similar to steam cooking.

   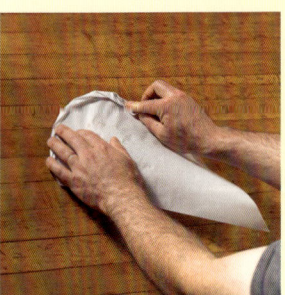

1. Trim fish and pat dry with paper towels.
2. Place fish skin-side down on a piece of oiled or buttered parchment or aluminum foil.
3. Add aromatic vegetables, a small quantity of liquid — fish stock (see recipe on page 21), citrus juice or white wine — and seal packet tightly.
4. Place in oven-safe casserole dish or on baking sheet.
5. Do not turn packet during cooking.
6. Bake in a 350°F oven.

CASSEROLE OR OPEN-PAN BAKING

This technique consists of oven-baking lake whitefish in a liquid such as court bouillon (see recipe on page 17) or fish stock (see recipe on page 21) with the addition of herbs and spices.

1. Place fish in an oiled or buttered pan.
2. Add herbs and spices.
3. Cover with a fish stock or court bouillon.
4. Bake at 350°F.
5. Baste frequently to prevent drying.

PAN ROASTING

This technique is used for cooking larger pieces of fish, such as a whole lake whitefish, that are too large to finish with other methods. There are two basic steps:

1. Sear the lake whitefish on the stove in a cast-iron skillet or roasting pan.
2. Finish in the oven uncovered until the flesh flakes with a fork.

Lake whitefish is generally roasted with fresh or dried herbs. Exactly which you use is up to you, but the list can include:

☐ Lemon or lime wedges
☐ Garlic
☐ Fresh thyme
☐ Fresh rosemary
☐ Fresh parsley
☐ Fresh ginger
☐ Wild leeks
☐ Olive oil
☐ Whatever else you prefer

HERBED WHITEFISH EN PAPILLOTE

Chef Chris Kibit

Yield: 2 servings
Prep Time: 20 minutes
Cook Time: 20 minutes

INGREDIENTS

☐ 2 Great Lakes whitefish fillets (6–8 ounces each)
☐ Pinch of salt
☐ 3 teaspoons chopped fresh chives
☐ 3 teaspoons chopped fresh dill
☐ 3 teaspoons minced shallots
☐ 6 button mushrooms, sliced
☐ ¾ cup diced fresh tomatoes
☐ Butter shavings
☐ 2 teaspoons fresh lemon juice
☐ 2 teaspoons white wine

Preparation

1. Preheat oven to 375°F.
2. Lay whitefish fillets on buttered parchment paper, cut into heart shape, large enough for 1 fillet to lie on 1 side (see photo on page 34).
3. Season with salt, fresh herbs and shallots.
4. Place sliced mushrooms on top and sprinkle with diced tomatoes.
5. Dot with butter shavings.
6. Sprinkle with lemon juice and wine.
7. Carefully bring half of paper over fish and fold, then crimp open edges to seal.
8. Place on baking sheet and bake for approximately 20 minutes, depending on the size of the fillet.

Note: This dish can be opened in the kitchen and served on rice or with roasted or boiled potatoes. You can also let your guest open it and enjoy the aroma firsthand. Clean-up is easy if you leave it in the paper and just toss the paper after dinner. Serve with lemon wedges and fresh dill for garnish.

TERIYAKI BACON-WRAPPED WHITEFISH

Chef Chris Sturzl

Yield: 6 servings
Prep Time: 20 minutes + 4 hours marinating time
Cook Time: 12 minutes

INGREDIENTS

- ☐ 6 Great Lakes whitefish fillets (6 ounces each)
- ☐ 6 strips of applewood-smoked bacon
- ☐ ½ cup soy sauce
- ☐ ¼ cup water
- ☐ 1 small fresh ginger root, peeled and sliced thin lengthwise
- ☐ 2 tablespoons brown sugar
- ☐ 1 clove garlic, minced

Procedure

1. Preheat oven to 350°F.
2. In a large bowl mix soy sauce, water, ginger, sugar and garlic for marinade.
3. Place whitefish fillets on baking pan.
4. Pour marinade over fillets. Work marinade around fillets.
5. Cover and place in refrigerator for 4 hours, rotating fillets once or twice during that time.
6. Remove fillets from marinade and wrap one slice of bacon around each so it lies flat. (The bacon might make only one or two revolutions around the fillet, so be sure to center it and put the fold on the bottom.)
7. Lay wrapped fillets on parchment paper or on a foil-lined baking sheet.
8. Bake for 12 minutes or until fillets reach an internal temp of 160°F.*
9. Serve hot.

Note: Serve alongside or on top of shredded red and green cabbage that has been flash fried (quickly sautéed with little oil and high heat) with pineapple and kiwi. Use wok oil seasoned with garlic, ginger, coriander and black pepper to flash fry, or stir fry on high heat.

Or try the following chutney.

INGREDIENTS FOR PINEAPPLE AND SWEET RED CHERRY CHUTNEY

- ☐ 1 cup chopped pineapple
- ☐ ½ cup pitted and chopped fresh sweet red cherries
- ☐ 1 tablespoon minced shallots
- ☐ ¼ cup chopped cilantro

Preparation

1. Stir all ingredients together with a spoon.

May also be grilled. Grill flesh-side down for 2 minutes then flip and finish grilling with skin-side down.

BAKED WHITEFISH ADRIATIC

Yield: 8 servings
Prep Time: 35 minutes
Cook Time: 35 minutes

INGREDIENTS

- ☐ 12 carrots, thinly sliced lengthwise
- ☐ 2 fresh tomatoes, chopped
- ☐ 4 green onions, chopped
- ☐ 12 black peppercorns, crushed
- ☐ 1 bay leaf
- ☐ ½ teaspoon dried oregano
- ☐ ½ teaspoon dried basil
- ☐ 1 cup white wine
- ☐ ½ cup clam juice or water
- ☐ ½ cup olive oil
- ☐ Juice of 2 fresh lemons
- ☐ ½ cup chopped fresh parsley
- ☐ Salt and pepper to taste
- ☐ 3 pounds skinless Great Lakes whitefish fillets
- ☐ 16 mussels, scrubbed and well washed
- ☐ 8 clams, scrubbed and well washed
- ☐ 16 medium shrimp, unshelled, slit and deveined (or substitute large cooked shrimp and add during the last 10 minutes of cooking)
- ☐ Lemon slices for garnish

Preparation

1. Preheat oven to 375°F.
2. Combine the first 11 ingredients plus ¼ cup of the parsley and salt in a bowl.
3. In a heavy baking pan, combine the shellfish and vegetable mixture.
4. Heat on top of stove for approximately 10 minutes or until the liquid is reduced, stirring frequently but gently.
5. Place in oven and bake uncovered for 20 minutes or until mussels and clams open. Discard those shells that do not open after 20 minutes.
6. Add whitefish (and shrimp, if cooked are used) in the last 10 minutes of cooking.
7. Remove fish, shellfish and bay leaf from pan and keep warm.
8. Simmer the liquid until reduced by half.
9. Check seasoning and adjust to taste.
10. Sprinkle with the remaining parsley; pour sauce over the fish and serve. Garnish with lemon slices.

PISTACHIO-CRUSTED GREAT LAKES WHITEFISH WITH CITRUS SPINACH SALAD

Chef Rajeev Patgaonkar

Yield: 4 servings
Prep Time: 30 minutes
Cook Time: 10 minutes

INGREDIENTS FOR WHITEFISH

- ☐ 1 cup dry breadcrumbs
- ☐ 6 tablespoons shelled pistachios, lightly toasted
- ☐ 2 tablespoons packed fresh parsley
- ☐ ½ teaspoon garlic powder
- ☐ 4 skinless Great Lakes whitefish fillets (3 ounces each)
- ☐ ½ teaspoon salt
- ☐ ¼ teaspoon ground black pepper
- ☐ ¼ cup nonfat plain (unsweetened) yogurt

INGREDIENTS FOR SALAD

- ☐ 1 pound raw baby spinach
- ☐ 12 orange segments
- ☐ 12 grapefruit segments
- ☐ ⅓ cup red onion, thinly sliced
- ☐ 12 grape tomatoes, cut in half (lengthwise)

INGREDIENTS FOR SALAD DRESSING

- ☐ Zest and juice of 1 orange
- ☐ Zest and juice of 1 lime
- ☐ 1 large shallot, quartered
- ☐ 2 teaspoons olive oil
- ☐ ½ teaspoon sea salt
- ☐ ¼ teaspoon ground black pepper
- ☐ ⅛ teaspoon cayenne pepper

Preparation

1. Heat oven to 400°F.
2. Purée salad dressing ingredients in blender or food processor to make dressing. Remove and set aside.
3. Pulse bread crumbs, nuts, parsley and garlic powder in food processor until nuts are roughly chopped.
4. Pour dry blend onto parchment paper.
5. Cut 3-ounce portions from whitefish fillets. Use remainder of fillets for spreads, soups or pasta.
6. Season whitefish with salt and pepper.
7. Coat tops of the fillets with yogurt.
8. Press the prepared breadcrumb blend into the tops of the fillets.
9. Place breadcrumb-side up on a baking sheet lined with parchment paper.
10. Bake until fish is no longer translucent in center, about 10 minutes. Finish under broiler for about 2 minutes.

Plating

1. Divide spinach among 4 plates.
2. Add thinly sliced red onion.
3. Place 6 halves of grape tomatoes and 3 each citrus segments, forming a triangle.
4. Drizzle each salad with 2 tablespoons of dressing.
5. Top it with baked whitefish fillet and serve.

DILL-BAKED WHITEFISH WITH TOMATO-CUCUMBER RELISH

This dish takes some work ahead of time, but is well worth the effort and will keep for up to 2 days once done. It will be served cold, so it's refreshing on a hot day.

Yield: 12 servings
Prep Time: 30 minutes + overnight 2 hours of chilling time
Cook Time: 20 minutes

INGREDIENTS FOR THE FISH

- ☐ Olive oil for brushing on pan
- ☐ 6 pounds fresh Great Lakes whitefish fillets
- ☐ 3 cups coarsely chopped fresh dill
- ☐ 1 medium onion, coarsely chopped
- ☐ 1 teaspoon coarse kosher salt
- ☐ ¼ teaspoon white pepper
- ☐ 6 tablespoons white vinegar

Preparation For Fish

1. Line heavy baking pan with foil and brush with oil.
2. Arrange fish skin-side down on foil.
3. In food processor, finely chop dill and onion.
4. Sprinkle each fillet with salt and pepper.
5. Press dill mixture onto fish.
6. Pour white vinegar evenly over the fish.
7. Cover and chill overnight, basting occasionally.
8. Preheat oven to 375°F.
9. Place baking pan on rack in center of oven.
10. Uncover fish and bake until just cooked through, about 15 minutes. Let the pan of fish cool.
11. Cover baked fish and chill at least 2 hours and up to 2 days.

INGREDIENTS FOR THE RELISH

- ☐ 4 cups diced, peeled, seeded cucumber (about 4)
- ☐ 2 pounds plum tomatoes (about 12), seeded and chopped
- ☐ ½ cup chopped fresh dill
- ☐ ¼ cup sherry vinegar
- ☐ 4 teaspoons coarse kosher salt
- ☐ Fresh dill sprigs for garnish

Preparation For Relish

1. Combine all of the ingredients in medium bowl and stir.
2. Let stand for 3 hours, stirring occasionally.
3. Check seasoning and adjust to your taste.

To Finish

1. Scrape most of the dill off the fish.
2. Cut crosswise into 12 portions, and trim neatly.
3. Slide spatula under each portion, separating it from the skin; dispose of skin.
4. Arrange fish on platter and spoon relish over. Serve cold, garnished with sprigs of fresh dill.

GREAT LAKES SUMMER WHITEFISH

Chef Deborah Pearce

Yield: 4 servings
Prep Time: 20 minutes
Cook Time: 20 minutes

INGREDIENTS FOR WHITEFISH

- ☐ 1 teaspoon sesame oil
- ☐ 12 arugula leaves
- ☐ 12 sorrel leaves
- ☐ 1½ pounds Great Lakes whitefish fillets
- ☐ 1¼ cups thinly sliced shiitake mushrooms

INGREDIENTS FOR RUB

- ☐ ½ cup fish sauce*
- ☐ 2 teaspoons minced fresh ginger
- ☐ 4 cloves fresh garlic, minced
- ☐ 1 tablespoon sesame seeds
- ☐ 6 scallions, thinly sliced
- ☐ ½ cup sesame oil
- ☐ ¼ cup fresh lime juice

Preparation

1. Preheat oven to 350°F.
2. Brush sesame oil on parchment paper (see photo demonstration on page 34) and layer arugula and sorrel on it.
3. Place whitefish on top of greens.

4. Mix fish sauce with ginger, garlic, sesame seeds, scallions, sesame oil and lime juice.

5. Let sit for 10 minutes.

6. Pour rub over fish; sprinkle with mushrooms.

7. Fold parchment paper, making sure it is sealed.

8. Place on baking sheet and bake for 20 minutes. Parchment will puff up and become golden brown when done.

9. Open parchment wrapper very carefully to avoid steam burn.

Note: This dish lends itself beautifully to being served in the paper (en Papillote), letting the diner cut into the parchment and getting the full impact. It looks great nestled on a bed of wild or brown rice or roasted red potatoes and served with a couple of lime wedges for extra color and citrus flavor. My guests have always enjoyed this unique presentation, and I love that you can just pick up the paper and dispose of it, nice and tidy.

Fish sauce has an unpleasant aroma, but that disappears and the sauce enhances the flavor of the fish tremendously.

GREAT LAKES WHITEFISH WITH VEGETABLE CONFETTI

This dish is simple, colorful and very healthy. Use fresh herbs if available; just double the quantities listed below. Your favorite potato dish will make an ideal side dish as will fresh or canned fruit.

Yield: 2 servings
Prep Time: 30 minutes
Cook Time: 10–12 minutes

INGREDIENTS

- ☐ 2 cubed, skinless Great Lakes whitefish fillets (8 ounces each)
- ☐ 1 teaspoon dried basil
- ☐ 1 teaspoon paprika
- ☐ Pinch of red pepper
- ☐ Pinch of black pepper
- ☐ 1 teaspoon salt
- ☐ 1 clove garlic, minced
- ☐ ½ cup chopped green onions
- ☐ 2 tablespoons chopped parsley
- ☐ ½ cup chopped and seeded tomatoes
- ☐ 2 cups diced red, yellow and green peppers
- ☐ 2 tablespoons butter
- ☐ ¼ cup olive or canola oil
- ☐ 2 tablespoons lemon juice

Preparation

1. Preheat oven to 350°F.
2. Combine basil, paprika, red pepper, black pepper and salt and set aside.
3. Put garlic, onion, parsley, tomato and peppers in a large bowl and set aside.
4. Pour oil into a 13"x 9"x 2" baking dish.
5. Spread half of vegetables in dish and sprinkle with half of spice mixture.
6. Place fish on top.
7. Spread remaining vegetables and spices on fish.
8. Cut butter into small pieces and place on top.
9. Sprinkle with lemon juice.
10. Bake uncovered on center oven rack for 10–12 minutes.
11. Push peppers to sides of dish and move dish to upper oven rack.
12. Broil for about 4 minutes or until fish flakes easily.

LASAGNA OCEANA

Yield: About 6 servings
Prep Time: 1½ hours
Cook Time: 45 minutes

INGREDIENTS FOR LASAGNA SAUCE

- ☐ 1 medium onion, chopped
- ☐ 2 garlic cloves, chopped
- ☐ 2 tablespoons oil
- ☐ 1 pound raw ground or cooked flaked Great Lakes whitefish
- ☐ 3½ cups canned tomatoes (1 pound, 12 ounce can)
- ☐ 1 can (6 ounces) tomato paste
- ☐ 2 cups water
- ☐ 1 tablespoon salt
- ☐ ⅛ teaspoon cayenne pepper
- ☐ Pinch of oregano
- ☐ 1 bay leaf

Sauce Preparation

1. Brown onion and garlic lightly in oil.
2. Add fish and cook until crumbly (several minutes for raw ground fish, only a couple for cooked flaked fish).
3. Add remaining sauce ingredients.
4. Simmer, uncovered for 1½ hours.
5. Remove bay leaf before using sauce.

INGREDIENTS FOR PASTA

- ☐ 8 ounces lasagna noodles
- ☐ 1 pound ricotta cheese
- ☐ 2 cups mozzarella cheese, sliced
- ☐ Lasagna sauce
- ☐ ½ cup grated Parmesan cheese

Preparation

1. Preheat oven to 325°F.
2. Cook noodles in boiling, salted water for about 25 minutes, or until tender. Drain.
3. Arrange in shallow 2½ quart baking dish, making 3 layers each of noodles, ricotta, mozzarella, sauce and Parmesan cheese.
4. Bake uncovered for about 45 minutes.

SAVORY BAKED WHITEFISH

Yield: 4 servings
Prep Time: 20 minutes
Cook Time: 15 minutes

INGREDIENTS

- ☐ 2 pounds skinless Great Lakes whitefish fillets
- ☐ 2 small onions, sliced
- ☐ 3 tablespoons olive oil
- ☐ Dash of kosher salt
- ☐ Dash of black pepper
- ☐ 1 clove garlic, minced or pressed
- ☐ 1½ tablespoons lemon juice
- ☐ 3 tablespoons white wine
- ☐ 1 cup heavy cream
- ☐ ½ teaspoon dried oregano leaves
- ☐ ⅓ cup grated cheddar cheese
- ☐ ⅓ cup grated Parmesan cheese
- ☐ 2 tablespoons dry white bread crumbs
- ☐ ½ pound cooked #20–25 shrimp, coarsely chopped

Preparation

1. Preheat oven to 425°F.
2. Sauté onion in olive oil in heavy pan over medium heat. Do not brown.
3. Spread onion over bottom of a shallow baking dish.
4. Arrange Great Lakes whitefish fillets over onion in pan, overlapping thin edges to prevent overcooking.
5. Sprinkle shrimp on top of fish.
6. Sprinkle with salt and pepper.
7. Add the garlic.
8. Pour wine or lemon juice over fish.
9. Add cream and oregano to the pan.
10. Cover with foil.
11. Bake for about 5 minutes.
12. Remove from oven and uncover.
13. Add cheddar cheese, Parmesan cheese and bread crumbs.
14. Bake, uncovered, for another 10 minutes or until top is golden, cheese is melted and fish flakes easily.

HOMESTYLE WHITEFISH LOAF

Gauthier & Spaulding Fisheries

Yield: 4–6 servings
Prep Time: 20 minutes
Cook Time: 1 hour

INGREDIENTS

- ☐ 1 pound ground raw or cooked flaked Great Lakes whitefish
- ☐ 2 tablespoons salad oil
- ☐ ¾ cup quick-cooking oats
- ☐ 2 eggs, beaten
- ☐ 1 cup chopped onions
- ☐ ½ package dry onion soup mix
- ☐ 2 teaspoons soy sauce, divided

Preparation

1. Preheat oven to 350°F.
2. Mix together all ingredients, except 1 teaspoon soy sauce.
3. Put into greased loaf pan, and pour remaining 1 teaspoon soy sauce over top.
4. Bake for about 1 hour.

SIMPLY BAKED WHITEFISH

This preparation is the ultimate in simplicity. Pair with one of the following uniquely flavored sauces — curry, fennel or traditional tartar — to suit your taste. See recipes on page 42.

Yield: 4 servings
Prep Time: 5 minutes
Cook Time: 15 minutes

INGREDIENTS

- ☐ 4 skinless, pin-boned Great Lakes whitefish fillets (8 ounces each)
- ☐ 2 teaspoons butter
- ☐ Salt and pepper to taste
- ☐ Lemon wedges

Preparation

1. Preheat oven to 375°F.
2. Cover a baking sheet with aluminum foil and spray with olive oil.
3. Place fillets on baking sheet.
4. Dot with butter and season with salt and pepper.
5. Bake 15 minutes until butter is melted and fish flesh is opaque.
6. Serve with lemon wedges or one of the suggested sauces.

CURRY SAUCE

Yield: 2 cups
Prep Time: 15 minutes
Cook Time: 5 minutes

INGREDIENTS

- ☐ 1 cup mayonnaise
- ☐ 1 cup sour cream
- ☐ 1 clove garlic, minced
- ☐ 2 teaspoons curry powder
- ☐ 3 tablespoons olive oil
- ☐ 3 tablespoons sugar
- ☐ Juice from 2 oranges
- ☐ 2 tablespoons fresh lemon juice
- ☐ 2 tablespoons mango chutney
- ☐ ½ teaspoon salt
- ☐ ½ teaspoon pepper
- ☐ 2 tablespoons gin

Preparation

1. Combine mayonnaise and sour cream in a medium bowl and set aside.
2. In a small pan, sauté garlic and curry powder in olive oil over low heat until well blended.
3. Remove from heat and stir into mayonnaise mixture.
4. Add sugar, orange and lemon juices, chutney, salt, pepper and gin.
5. Blend with an immersion (stick) blender until smooth.
6. Chill.

SIMPLE TARTAR SAUCE

Yield: 1 cup
Prep Time: 5 minutes

INGREDIENTS

- ☐ 1 tablespoon chopped onions
- ☐ 1 cup mayonnaise
- ☐ 1 tablespoon chopped dill pickle
- ☐ ½ teaspoon granulated garlic

Preparation

Mix ingredients well. Chill before serving.

FENNEL SAUCE

Yield: 1 quart
Prep Time: 20 minutes
Cook Time: 30 minutes

INGREDIENTS

- ☐ ½ cup all-purpose flour
- ☐ ½ stick butter, melted
- ☐ 1 quart fish stock (see recipe on page 21)
- ☐ 1 small bunch of fresh fennel
- ☐ 1 tablespoon butter
- ☐ 2 shallots, chopped
- ☐ ¼ cup white wine
- ☐ ½ cup heavy cream, warmed
- ☐ Salt and pepper to taste

Preparation

1. Make a roux (thickener) by combining the flour and melted butter with a whisk in a sauce pan.
2. Cook, stirring on medium heat for 3–4 minutes until roux starts to thicken and turn brown.
3. Add stock to roux, whisking vigorously. Make sure both roux and stock are not hot – have one cooled down to combine.
4. Steam the leafy green part of the fennel for 2 minutes and add to stock.
5. Simmer 20 minutes.
6. In a separate pan, sauté shallots in butter, add wine and reduce.
7. Add warmed cream to wine mixture and reduce again.
8. Add this mixture to stock and fennel.
9. Purée and strain.
10. Cook the bulb of the fennel in small amount of liquid for 6–10 minutes until it is fork tender. Cut the bulb into strips. Use lemon juice to keep it white. Use for garnish.

CHAPTER SIX
SMOKING AND PICKLING

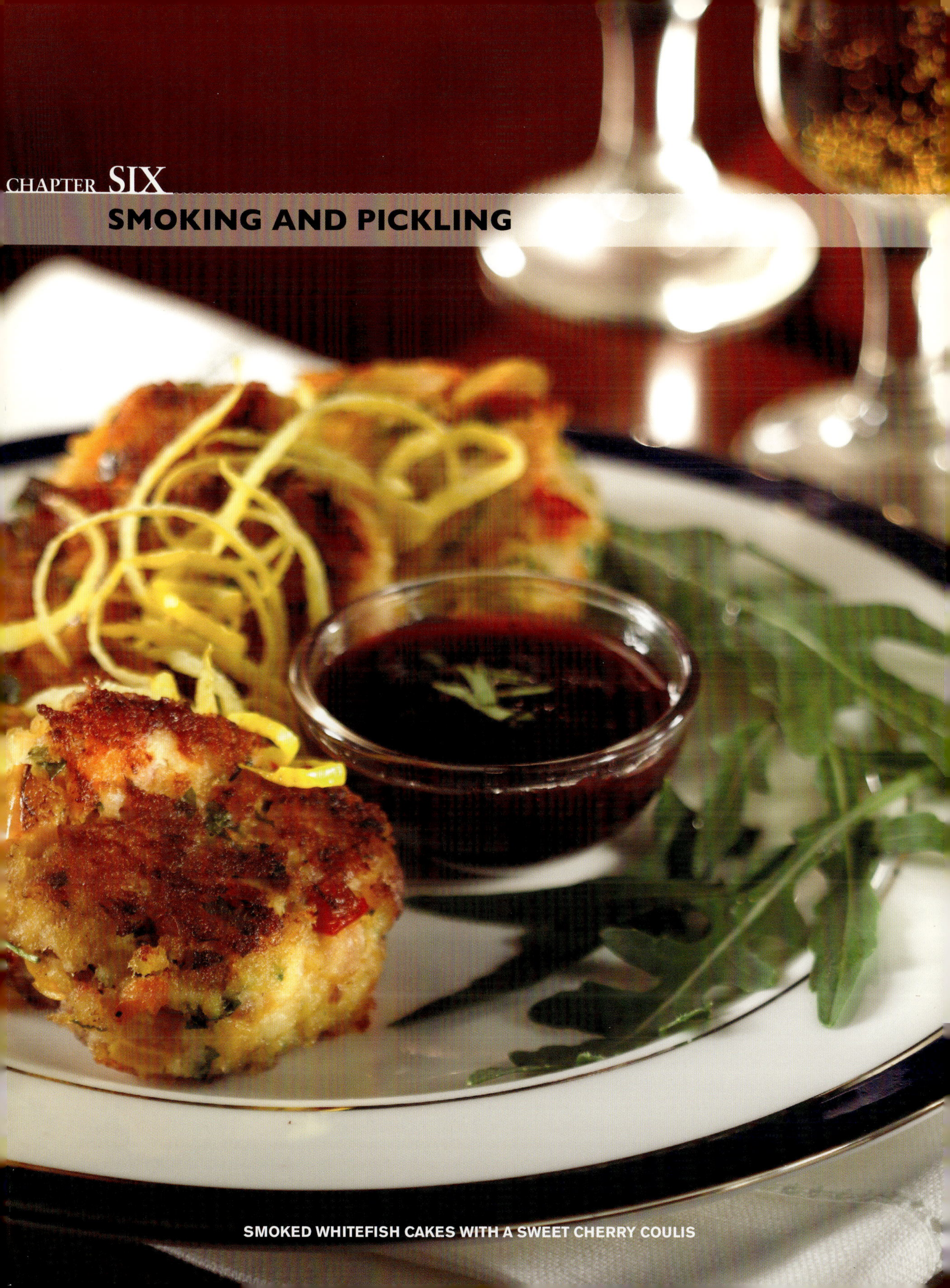

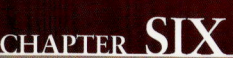

SMOKED WHITEFISH CAKES WITH A SWEET CHERRY COULIS

Smoking and Pickling Techniques

Smoking and pickling techniques can be applied to lake whitefish as both an initial cooking procedure to add flavor and as a method of preservation.

SMOKING

Equipment

☐ Smoker
☐ Pans for wood and liquid (often provided with commercial smokers)
☐ Hardwood
☐ Thermometer

There are two basic smoking methods — cold and hot. Cold smoking is done mainly by commercial processors, so we will concentrate on hot smoking. Smoking lake whitefish can be easy if you follow some basic steps. All you need is a smoker, heat, brine, hardwood and some fish. Most varieties of fish can be smoked.

Smoking can be done in any kind of enclosure in which the air can be regulated — kettle grills, electric smokers and water smokers, to name a few. Commercially sold products include smoker boxes, which hold soaked wood chips and can be put over the hot part of a grill to create a smoky flavor in food while grilling.

Maintaining uniform heat at 180°F in the smoking enclosure for the total smoking period is important. Cooking the fish to an internal temperature of 145°F and maintaining it for 30 minutes is also very important. Water-smoking whitefish prevents excessive drying. In this method, place a pan of water or other liquid (beer, wine, etc.) above the heated wood chips, which will produce steam, thus keeping the fish moist.

The wood should be a good hardwood, never a soft, resinous one such as pine. Likewise, do not use leftover construction materials or creosote-treated wood to fuel the fire. Although which wood is "best" is a debate, the following are the most commonly used.

ALDER: Indigenous to the Pacific Northwest, Native American tribes in that area developed alder-smoked salmon into an art form. Alder has a light, delicate smoke that is perfect for fish.

APPLE: Apple wood has a slightly sweet, fruity smoke.

CHERRY: Like apple, cherry is a sweeter smoke and great with fish and most meats.

HICKORY: The most commonly used wood, hickory is great for all types of barbecues.

MAPLE: Maple provides a mild smoke that works with most foods.

MESQUITE: In Texas, ranchers used to pay people to haul away the mesquite shrub. That changed with the discovery that mesquite was great for barbecuing. It burns very hot, so is more suited for grilling than smoking.

OAK: Oak has a mild smoke that complements a variety of foods, especially beef.

PECAN: The new "hot" flavor in woods, pecan provides a mild, mellow smoke that works on anything.

All woods may be soaked for several hours in a liquid (not oil) prior to use.

PICKLING

Equipment

- Bowl or crock made of a non-reactive material
- Plate and some sort of weight to keep fish submerged
- Strainer
- Jars for storage

Pickling is an easy method of preserving lake whitefish. Pickled fish must be stored in the refrigerator at no higher than 40°F (refrigerator temperature) and for best flavor must be used within 4–6 weeks. Almost any type of fish may be pickled at home. The necessary ingredients are:

- Water – Avoid hard water as it causes off color and flavors.
- Vinegar containing at least 5% acetic acid. Do not use apple cider vinegar, wine vinegar or homemade vinegar.
- Pickling salt
- Spices
- Fish – May have been frozen, then thawed before pickling.
- Refrigeration – Fish must be refrigerated during all stages of the pickling process.

GREAT LAKES WHITEFISH CAVIAR

These beautiful, small, crunchy, slightly salty fish eggs are a delicacy that must be experienced. Many whitefish lovers are unaware of the delectable addition that caviar can make to finish a dish. Most recipes in this book would benefit from a small dollop of caviar as a garnish or stirred into a sauce at the very end for an interesting touch of color and texture.

Whitefish caviar can also stand alone as a unique and elegant appetizer. Simply place a small amount of sour cream or softened cream cheese on a cracker of your choice and top with ¼ teaspoon of caviar, garnish with a sliver of chive, and your guests will be thrilled. Get creative with this little-used product and see what you can come up with.

You will have to ask your local fish house if they carry caviar. It is usually not expensive. My fishmonger keeps it in the freezer and almost always has it in stock.

Enjoy!

Deb Pearce

GREAT LAKES MUFFALETTA

Chef Eric Villegas

Yield: Serves 6–8
Prep Time: 1 hour + overnight resting
Cook Time: 1 hour + 20 minutes if serving hot

INGREDIENTS

☐ 1 large red onion, peeled and thinly sliced
☐ 1 cup cooked artichoke hearts packed in oil, drained well and thinly sliced
☐ ½ cup roasted bell peppers
☐ ½ cup capers
☐ ⅓ cup red wine vinegar
☐ Sea salt to taste
☐ Black pepper freshly ground, to taste
☐ 1 teaspoon vinegar
☐ 4 whole eggs
☐ 1 large artisan focaccia loaf
☐ ½ cup Basil Walnut Pesto (see recipe on page 47)
☐ 2 cups romaine lettuce, shredded
☐ 4 fresh cow's milk mozzarella balls, sliced
☐ 4 heirloom tomatoes, sliced
☐ 12 ounces smoked Great Lakes whitefish, boned and flaked
☐ 8 white anchovy fillets or similar, drained

Preparation

1. In a small bowl, combine the sliced onions, artichoke, bell peppers, capers and red wine vinegar.
2. Mix well and set aside for at least 15 minutes for the flavors to meld and the onions to wilt.
3. Hard boil the eggs, starting with cold water and a teaspoon of vinegar in a small saucepan. Bring to a boil and cook for 3 minutes. Remove from heat and let the eggs remain in the hot water for 10 minutes. Peel, slice and set aside.
4. Slice the focaccia in half horizontally.
5. Spread the pesto evenly between top and bottom.

6. Start with the bottom half of the focaccia, cover it with the shredded romaine lettuce, followed by the fresh mozzarella cheese, artichoke/onion mixture and tomato slices.
7. Season the tomatoes with some salt and pepper.
8. Follow with smoked whitefish, sliced hard-boiled eggs and finish with the anchovy fillets.
9. Cover the muffaletta with the reserved top of the focaccia.
10. Wrap the sandwich very tightly in plastic wrap, then overwrap tightly in foil.
11. Store overnight in the refrigerator topped with a heavy skillet, heavy plate or even a brick to compress.
12. Remove from refrigerator, slice and serve.
13. This sandwich can be heated in foil (with plastic removed) before serving if a hot sandwich is preferred.

INGREDIENTS FOR ROASTED GARLIC PURÉE

☐ 1 pound fresh whole garlic heads, or similar
☐ ½ cup extra virgin cold pressed olive oil
☐ Sea salt to taste
☐ Black pepper freshly ground, to taste
☐ Fresh rosemary sprigs

To Roast the Garlic

1. Preheat the oven to 375°F.
2. Peel the outermost layers of skin off the heads of garlic, leaving an intact whole head free of any scrap. Split the heads in half cutting across the equator, opening the cloves.
3. Put the heads cut-side up in a small baking dish and pour the olive oil over them.
4. Season with salt, pepper, and top with the rosemary.
5. Cover tightly with foil or lid, place in the oven, and roast until about ¾ cooked, about 45 minutes.
6. Uncover and return to the oven until the cloves begin to pop out of their skins and brown, about 15 minutes.

To Make a Purée

1. When cool enough to handle easily, squeeze the roasted garlic into a small bowl.
2. Press firmly against the skins to extract as much of the sweet roasted garlic as you can.
3. Add the oil from the baking dish and purée with the back of a spoon or in a small food processor until a paste forms.

INGREDIENTS FOR BASIL WALNUT PESTO

- ☐ 2 cups fresh basil leaves, firmly packed
- ☐ 1 tablespoon Roasted Garlic Purée (see recipe above)
- ☐ Sea salt to taste
- ☐ Black pepper freshly ground, to taste
- ☐ ⅓ cup extra virgin, cold-pressed olive oil
- ☐ 3 tablespoons toasted walnuts
- ☐ ¼ cup shaved Parmesan cheese for serving
- ☐ ¼ cup freshly squeezed lime juice

Preparation

1. Prepare an ice water bath in a large bowl.
2. Bring a large pot of water to boil.
3. Put the basil in a large sieve and blanch the herb by plunging it into the boiling water.
4. Cook for about 15 seconds.
5. Remove the basil; shake off the excess water, then plunge it immediately into the ice water bath, stirring quickly so it cools as rapidly as possible. Drain well.
6. Squeeze the water out of the basil with your hands until very dry.
7. Rough chop the basil and put in a blender or smaller food processor.
8. Add Roasted Garlic Purée, salt and pepper to taste, olive oil, walnuts.
9. Blend for at least 30 seconds.
10. Add the cheese and pulse to combine.

NORWEGIAN PICKLED WHITEFISH

Yield: 4 pounds pickled fish
Prep Time: 25 minutes
Cook Time: 5 minutes + 1 hour cooling time

INGREDIENTS

- ☐ 4 pounds skinless, pin-boned Great Lakes whitefish fillets, cut into 1-inch cubes
- ☐ 1 large onion, thinly sliced
- ☐ 2 tablespoons fresh dill
- ☐ ¼ cup water
- ☐ ¼ cup vinegar (at least 5% acetic acid)
- ☐ 1 cup dry white wine (or sweet if you prefer a sweeter finished product)
- ☐ 1 teaspoon minced garlic
- ☐ 1 teaspoon whole coriander seed
- ☐ 1 tablespoon Dijon style mustard
- ☐ Salt and pepper to taste

Preparation

1. Preheat oven to 375°F.
2. Place the whitefish in a baking dish just large enough to hold the fillets comfortably.
3. Spread the onions over the top and set aside.
4. Combine mustard, coriander, garlic, wine, vinegar, water, dill, salt and pepper in a small pot.
5. Quickly bring the mixture to a boil over high heat and pour immediately over the whitefish fillets.
6. Cover the baking dish and place in the oven for 5 minutes.
7. Remove fish from the oven, let it cool to room temperature, and place it in the refrigerator to cool completely.
8. Serve chilled with onions and some pickling liquid.

Note: Will keep up to 2 weeks under appropriate refrigeration.

MIDDLE ISLAND POINT SMOKED WHITEFISH

Philip Pearce

Yield: About 3 pounds of edible Great Lakes whitefish, either whole or fillets
Prep Time: 3 hours (including brining time)
Cook Time: 3 hours

INGREDIENTS

- ☐ 1 whole whitefish – about 4 pounds (use only fresh Great Lakes whitefish or fish that was frozen quickly while fresh)

Brine

- ☐ 8 cups water
- ☐ 8 cups beer
- ☐ 1½ cups kosher salt
- ☐ 2 large sprigs fresh thyme (or lemon thyme)
- ☐ 1 sprig rosemary
- ☐ 10 cloves of garlic, smashed

Preparation

1. Clean the fish, removing the head, tail, fins, etc.
2. Remove any bruised or damaged flesh.
3. Wash in clean water.
4. Prepare brine of 2½ tablespoons plain salt to 1 cup of water. You need 1 quart of brine (10 tablespoons of salt to 32 ounces water) for every pound of fish.
5. Place fish in brine for 2–2½ hours.
6. Prepare smoker according to manufacturer's directions.
7. Plan on smoking for 3 hours per pound of fish.
8. Remove fish from brine and rinse with cold water.
9. Place fish skin-side down on oiled smoker rack.
10. Keep the temperature low, around 150°F.
11. Increase heat after the first 2 hours to around 200°F.
12. Continue smoking until fish is flaky and cooked through, testing every 30 minutes to see if it's done.
13. Serve immediately or refrigerate. If you don't plan to eat the fish in a couple of days, wrap it tightly and put it in the freezer.

ROY AND ALICE'S PICKLED FISH

Gauthier & Spaulding Fisheries

Yield: 1 pound Great Lakes whitefish
Prep Time: 15 minutes
Cook Time: 10 minutes

INGREDIENTS

- ☐ 1 pound Great Lakes whitefish fillets
- ☐ 1 medium onion, sliced
- ☐ 2–3 bay leaves
- ☐ ¾ teaspoon salt

Pickling vinegar

- ☐ 1 cup vinegar (at least 5% acetic)
- ☐ ½ cup water
- ☐ ½ teaspoon salt
- ☐ 1 tablespoon sugar
- ☐ 2 teaspoons whole mixed pickling spices
- ☐ 2 tablespoons salad oil

Preparation

1. Wash fillets and drain.
2. Sprinkle salt over fish.
3. Arrange fish in steamer dish and steam 3–5 minutes or until fish flakes.
4. Lift out fillets and arrange in jar or small crock with onions and bay leaves.
5. Heat all pickling vinegar ingredients to a boil.
6. Simmer 10 minutes and strain.
7. Add salad oil.
8. Pour mixture over fish.
9. Cover and refrigerate before using.

Note: Fish will keep in a cold refrigerator for 4–6 weeks.

SMOKED WHITEFISH DIP WITH ALE

Chef Jeffrey Kudrna

Yield: 1 pound
Prep Time: 20 minutes
Cook Time: 15 minutes

INGREDIENTS

- ☐ 1 pound smoked whitefish, skin and bones removed
- ☐ ½ large white onion, diced
- ☐ 3 sprigs fresh dill
- ☐ ½ cup mayonnaise
- ☐ ½ cup sour cream
- ☐ ¼ cup of your favorite ale
- ☐ Salt to taste
- ☐ Shredded Parmesan cheese

Preparation

1. Place the diced onion in a hot pan with oil until caramelized and set aside.
2. In a food processor, add the whitefish, caramelized onion, sprigs of dill, mayonnaise and sour cream. Purée the mixture.
3. When smooth, add the ale.
4. Make sure mixture has a smooth consistency.
5. Add salt to taste.
6. Place mixture in an oven-safe bowl and sprinkle Parmesan cheese on top.
7. Place under broiler until cheese is brown.
8. Serve with crackers or toasted flat bread.

THILL'S FISH HOUSE SMOKED WHITEFISH SPREAD

Ted Thill

A very popular appetizer at many cocktail parties and gatherings in the Marquette area.

Yield: About 1 pound
Prep Time: 25–30 minutes
Cook Time: None

INGREDIENTS

- ☐ 1 pound smoked Great Lakes whitefish (a combination of different smoked fish can be used)
- ☐ 1½ cups real mayonnaise
- ☐ 1 cup sweet relish
- ☐ ½ cup small diced onions

Preparation

1. Remove fish bones and flake the flesh into small pieces.
2. Mix mayonnaise, relish and onions.
3. Add mixture to the flaked whitefish and let sit in refrigerator for at least 1 hour before serving.

Note: Properly refrigerated, the spread will keep for up to 10 days.

SMOKED WHITEFISH CAKES WITH A SWEET CHERRY COULIS

Chef Darlene Kline

Yield: 4–6 servings
Prep Time: 1 hour
Cook Time: 10 minutes

INGREDIENTS

- ☐ 3 large fresh jalapeño peppers
- ☐ 2 tablespoons olive oil
- ☐ 1 medium red bell pepper, finely diced
- ☐ 1 medium yellow bell pepper, finely diced
- ☐ ½ cup plain bread crumbs
- ☐ ¾ cup mayonnaise
- ☐ ¼ cup coarsely chopped fresh cilantro
- ☐ 2 tablespoons favorite seafood seasoning
- ☐ 2 tablespoons minced garlic
- ☐ Black pepper to taste
- ☐ 1½ pounds smoked whitefish

Preparation

1. Preheat oven to 350°F.
2. Place jalapeños on oven rack and roast until skin is dark, 15–20 minutes.
3. Place jalapeños in a covered bowl and let rest 20 minutes.
4. Peel skin from peppers, remove seeds and finely chop.
5. Sauté the bell peppers in the olive oil until al dente. Set aside.
6. Combine breadcrumbs, mayonnaise, cilantro, seafood seasoning and garlic.
7. Add bell peppers and jalapeños, mix well.
8. Remove bones from fish, leaving chunks of fish if possible.
9. Gently fold fish into pepper mixture. Refrigerate for 20 minutes.
10. Preheat griddle to medium heat.
11. Scoop fish mixture into pan with a large ice cream scoop.
12. Flatten out with fingers to 1 inch thickness. Mixture will be crumbly.
13. Grill until lightly golden brown on each side, about 5–7 minutes.
14. Top with cherry coulis and serve warm.

CHERRY COULIS

I have only made this using 7 pounds of cherries at once, but the extra is great on ice cream, cannoli, pancakes etc.

INGREDIENTS

- ☐ 7 pounds fresh or frozen dark sweet cherries, pitted
- ☐ ½ cup corn syrup
- ☐ ¼ cup tart cherry juice concentrate
- ☐ Liquid fruit pectin
- ☐ Lemon juice

Preparation

1. Gently simmer all ingredients for 15 minutes.
2. Strain cherries through strainer, crushing out all the juice from the cherries.
3. Discard pulp.
4. Return juice to heat and simmer until reduced by ⅓ volume. Sauce should be slightly thick.
5. If you are in a hurry, add a couple envelopes of liquid fruit pectin to help thicken. If too thick, add lemon juice.

MUSTARD DILL SAUCE

Jill Bentgen

For smoked whitefish fillets and sausages.

Yield: 1 cup
Prep time: 10 minutes

Ingredients

- ☐ ½ cup mayonnaise
- ☐ ½ sour cream
- ☐ ¼ cup good, fruity mustard
- ☐ 2 tablespoons freshly squeezed lemon juice or more to taste
- ☐ 2 tablespoons fresh dill or more to taste

Preparation

1. Mix above ingredients together and refrigerate until use.

SMOKED WHITEFISH SALAD

Chef Cynthia Manning

This dish has been a favorite at the Governor's Mansion on Mackinac Island.

Yield: About 2 cups
Prep Time: 30 minutes
Cook Time: None

INGREDIENTS

- ☐ ½ whole smoked whitefish (about 2 pounds – see note)
- ☐ ¾ cup mayonnaise
- ☐ 1 tablespoon freshly squeezed lemon juice
- ☐ ¼ cup finely chopped green onions
- ☐ 2 tablespoons fresh dill

Preparation

1. Place the onions in a small bowl and cover with cold water. Let soak for 15 minutes. Drain.
2. Meanwhile, using a small knife and your hands, remove the skin, bones, and any brown bits from the whitefish and discard.
3. Flake the whitefish into small pieces into a medium bowl, checking again for any bones.
4. Add the onion to the whitefish and mix together with a fork.
5. Stir in the mayonnaise and lemon juice. For a smoother textured salad, pulse the whitefish mixture in a food processor.
6. Add dill and pepper to taste.
7. Serve immediately or store in the refrigerator for up to 3 days.

Note: If you're buying cleaned whitefish, you'll need 3⅓ cups.

SMOKED GREAT LAKES WHITEFISH AND ARTICHOKE DIP

Chef Robin Holmes

Yield: 2 pounds
Prep Time: 20 minutes
Cook Time: 10 minutes

INGREDIENTS

- ☐ 1 pound smoked whitefish, picked clean of bones, scales and skin
- ☐ 1 pound cream cheese, softened
- ☐ 1 cup sour cream
- ☐ ¼ cup mayonnaise
- ☐ ½ cup buttermilk
- ☐ 1 cup canned artichokes, rinsed and chopped
- ☐ ½ cup cooked spinach, squeezed dry in paper towel and chopped
- ☐ ¼ cup chopped green onions
- ☐ ½ tablespoon granulated garlic or garlic powder
- ☐ ¼ tablespoon granulated onion or onion powder
- ☐ ¼ tablespoon lemon pepper

Preparation

1. Thoroughly mix all ingredients together.
2. Place in a large oven-proof casserole dish or several individual oven-proof bowls.
3. Place in 375°F oven and cook until bubbling, about 10 minutes.
4. Serve with crackers or bread crisps.

SMOKED FISH PASTA SALAD

Jill Bentgen

Yield: 8 servings
Prep Time: 40 minutes
Cook Time: 15 minutes

INGREDIENTS

- ☐ 2 medium cucumbers
- ☐ 1 pound small pasta shells
- ☐ 2 tablespoons olive oil
- ☐ ½ cup thinly sliced scallions
- ☐ 1½ pound Great Lakes whitefish or lake trout fillet, smoked, skinned and broken into large flakes
- ☐ 2 tablespoons chopped fresh dill
- ☐ ¼ cup fresh parsley, chopped
- ☐ Lemon Caper Dressing (see following recipe)

Preparation

1. Peel, seed and thinly slice the cucumbers.
2. Place in a bowl of ice water for at least 30 minutes.
3. Cook pasta in salt water until al dente. Drain.
4. Refresh with cold water and drain thoroughly.
5. Pour pasta into a large bowl and toss with 2 tablespoons of a good fruity olive oil.
6. Drain the cucumbers thoroughly and add to cooked pasta.
7. Add fish, onions, dill, parsley and dressing to pasta.
8. Mix well.
9. Season to taste with salt and white pepper.

Note: Scoop onto a large platter lined with crisp lettuce leaves. Garnish with sprigs of fresh dill.

LEMON CAPER DRESSING

Yield: 1½ cups
Prep Time: 5 minutes

INGREDIENTS

- ☐ 1 cup mayonnaise
- ☐ ½ cup sour cream
- ☐ 1 teaspoon lemon zest
- ☐ Dash Tabasco sauce
- ☐ 1 tablespoon fresh lemon juice
- ☐ 3 tablespoons drained and rinsed capers

Preparation

1. Gently whisk together all ingredients, except capers, until smooth.
2. Stir in capers.
3. Chill until ready to use.

Note: This dressing is also good with fresh salmon that has been grilled or poached.

WHITEFISH LIVER SPREAD

This is a great appetizer for cocktail parties or a savory bite just before dinner. Serve with crusty French bread or crackers.

Yield: About 1 pound of finished spread
Prep Time: 15 minutes
Cook Time: 10 minutes

INGREDIENTS

- ☐ 3 tablespoons butter
- ☐ ¾ pound Great Lakes whitefish livers
- ☐ ⅓ cup finely chopped onion
- ☐ ⅓ cup water or dry white wine
- ☐ ¾ teaspoon garlic salt
- ☐ ¾ teaspoon salt
- ☐ ¼ teaspoon white pepper
- ☐ ¾ teaspoon paprika

Preparation

1. Heat the butter in a medium-size sauté pan until it begins to brown.
2. Add the livers and onion and sauté until they are cooked all the way through, about 8–10 minutes depending on the size of the livers.
3. Add the seasonings and stir.
4. Cool a few minutes.
5. Mix in a blender at medium speed until smooth.